TRANSITIONS IN CONNECTICUT

BILINGUAL EDUCATION IN THE WINDHAM PUBLIC SCHOOLS

JEAN ROMANO

iUNIVERSE, INC.
BLOOMINGTON

Transitions In Connecticut
Bilingual Education in the Windham Public Schools

iUniverse books may be ordered through booksellers or by contacting:

iUniverse
1663 Liberty Drive
Bloomington, IN 47403
www.iuniverse.com
1-800-Authors (1-800-288-4677)

ISBN: 978-1-4502-7965-9 (sc)
ISBN: 978-1-4502-7966-6 (ebk)

Printed in the United States of America

iUniverse rev. date: 2/17/2011

ACKNOWLEDGEMENTS

My beliefs and ideas on bilingual education and dual language programs come from many writers, historians, and researchers in the field. I am listing those that influenced me at the start of my studies in second language learning.

Some of the concepts are comprehensible input, as explained by Stephen Krashen, and James Cummins for explaining well the difference between social and academic language. Edward De Avila gave perspective on the assessment of English language proficiency and ways to measure it to properly place English language learners.

The progress of second language learners was best clarified through the research of Collier and Thomas who were able to give educators the understanding of the time needed to become fully bilingual. Kenji Hakuta also worked tirelessly on many projects to support the needs of second language learners. James Crawford has been the historian of bilingual programs and the politics affecting it.

Credit goes to Deborah Short and Jana Echevarria for bringing a system of teaching most likely to fuse the goals of language and content.

Donna Christian has all my thanks for assisting in the initiation of the Dual Language Program in Windham. This was done through the work and documentation of dual language programs across the country by the Center for Applied Linguistics and through her support at Windham's presentation to educators across the state.

For Piri Thomas, who spoke to my students and their parents about the experiences he had growing up in Spanish Harlem and how he overcame them.And, last but surely not least, Samuel Betances for his humor in spreading the positive messages of diversity.

Although they were not formally trained professional development educators in the field, my own learning transitions were the results of working with the students and teachers in the Windham Public Schools. Thank you all.

PREFACE

This brief history covers the time I was employed in the Windham Public Schools as a paraprofessional, ESL teacher, Bilingual Program Director and Title VII Project Director in that order. The years from the early '70's to the close of the '90's were exciting and full of hope. The English language learners themselves generated changes and improvements in bilingual education. The students who learned English in Windham were an inspiration. They survived the difficult transition from one set of values, history and traditions to another that often was not warm and welcoming. New arrivals to the public schools came from pre-school to high school. Most were citizens of the United States of America.

It would be a pleasure to report that there has been steady progress in addressing the issue of non-English speakers in the mainland schools. In some cases, public education has moved back to the policies of the '50's before the passage of the 1964 Civil Rights Act put a legal face on the inequality of classroom practices. It was many years ago, based on a suit brought by the Chinese community in San Francisco, that the goal of learning only English in school was not equality of opportunity. As a country, we need to revisit that ruling.

The last four decades produced a wealth of research to guide practitioners. It also brought new laws and mandates in many States ending bilingual education in favor of English only. The fear of foreign influence is a recurrent theme in our history. We now are at risk of losing the children who could help make ours a truly great nation.

What should be remembered in the debates about educating second language speakers is that those children traveling easily between Puerto Rico and mainland schools are citizens of the USA. While many English language learners are here while their parents study in our Universities, they intend to return to their countries of origin. Our Puerto Rican children may come and go with all the consequences of interrupted educational programs. They have skills, attitudes and values that can positively affect us all.

Indeed, all the second language learners bring new perspectives to their classmates. The strength of the USA is in the multitude of insights, cultures, traditions and ideals that are synthesized in communities across the nation.

CONTENTS

PART I

TEACHING

The Secret of Teaching is to appear to have known all your life what you have learned this afternoon.

Unknown

Beginnings

My family moved to Connecticut from Cincinnati, Ohio where I began my teaching career. As a mature student (read older than most) I worked towards certification at the University of Cincinnati. Burton Elementary was my assigned school for student teaching. There were one or two white children in the school but it was in an all black neighborhood and the community was proud to have a black principal in charge of their children's education. It was an experience to remember and I do. An atmosphere of confidence filled the building, teachers, parents and staff were sure each boy or girl would succeed and go on to the citywide college preparatory high school entered by passing a fairly stiff test. Many did pass and go on to Walnut Hills High School.

When we came to Connecticut we found a house in Mansfield where there is a state forest, a historic climbing rock and trails holding the presence of Native Americans. It was a full change from urban Cincinnati and the right place to bring three boys. Homes were set far apart and dairies formed a background for the houses. My children took full advantage of the freedom offered starting a life-long love of fishing, skiing, running, and hiking.

Willimantic, the neighboring small city, thrives in the center of this forested land. Two miles separate Mansfield and Willimantic but the culture and setting of these distinct parts of the Quiet Corner are very different. After talking to educators from the University of Connecticut and at Eastern Connecticut State University, I set my sights on a position in Willimantic. My training so far had been with urban schools; my student teaching in Burton Elementary School in Avondale, a part of the city that was mostly black and also the location of the city-wide college prep high school. Burton was proud of its rigorous standards. Willimantic seemed a better direction for me to take.

The Windham Public Schools looked less of a challenge than city schools in Cincinnati until I made the connection with English language learners during my early entrance into the district as a substitute. I was lucky to start a more settled position as a paraprofessional to the English as a Second Language Teacher (ESL) in Noble School and then moved on to Sweeney as a roving ESL teacher. It wasn't Burton but it was a fit for me.

Just having the opportunity to be part of another culture is still a fascination. My own background seemed imbedded in codfish cakes with stewed tomatoes. My husband's parents brought the good taste of Italy to my life and home cooking expanded to the staples of my mother-in-law's kitchen. It was time to learn the complexities of the Latin community.

The years in Windham were a learning experience from the first day. I am grateful for the students, teachers and administrators who supported me throughout those years.

The ESL program at Noble used the pull out system. Five or six students at a time came to the ESL room from a mainstream classroom. Their entrance to the support class often came under protest because ESL was scheduled at the expense of the fun activities planned for their classmates. There was no curriculum or lessons from the sending teachers. The boys and girls had varying degrees of need from no English to an English vocabulary that allowed them to function socially but not academically. The specific problems that labeled them as limited English proficient (LEP) were ours to find. The Connecticut Mastery Tests were far in the future; the standardized test for the district was the CTBS (California Test of Basic Skills). How much content in that test mirrored instruction and student background in Connecticut was a concern well above my knowledge bank and few educators questioned the efficacy of standardized tests. The youngest children came with no records at all. We gathered books, played games, read stories and did homework. Most of the classroom stories were not of interest; videos were non-existent for educational purposes. We talked loudly and made the ESL class as accepting and open a class as possible.

As an introduction to ESL, it was excellent. And an aide can't do too much harm in forty-five minutes a day. This was 1973 when research was non-existent and very few had a clue. Watching a third grade student read beautifully was puzzling. Jesus was an excellent reader only stumbling over pronunciation. His recall was exceptional. If asked a question about the story he could bring back the exact words in the book. It took some time to realize that comprehension was not attached to meaning and his limited vocabulary did not permit a choice of explanations. Mainstream teachers were shocked by the scores on reading tests for children like Jesus who seemed to be reading with ease. I asked Jesus' teacher what could be done to help him build his vocabulary. She felt that he showed himself to be at home with English on the playground and in class. His lack of progress must be a lack of motivation or a possible learning disability. Don't fault the teacher! None of us realized the needs of second language learners.

Nelson was a first grade student with abundant energy. He had learned a sure method for leaving the room. "I NEED to go baño," sounded real to me. And so he would be released to walk two doors down to the boy's bathroom. In a few days, administrators came looking for a child who had been out of the room at 9:45, 10:20 or any particular time of a specific day. Nelson's pattern fit those times. His need was to unwind as many toilet paper rolls as possible and run them through the building, leaving a trail of white in halls, on stairs and over doorknobs. Nelson was the not so secret skulker and his fun activity ended.

The children I met that year were able to function by taking every cue from English speaking classmates. Eduardo, Jesus, Magdaliz, Nelson and Juan: everyone a winner. They corrected my Spanish, cooperated with each lesson prepared and made my career decision to specialize in English language learners.

I lacked four credits to complete an M.A. in elementary education at the University of Cincinnati; The University of Connecticut accepted none of my credits. It was a good time to make a change and so I enrolled in the Master's program in Teaching English to Speakers of Other Languages/Curriculum and Instruction at the University of Connecticut. Dr. John Leach was my advisor then and a close friend until his death in 2008. It was the best career move I ever made. A job opening was posted for Sweeney Elementary School. I applied. And so I joined the ranks of ESL teachers who were untrained but dedicated, research and materials poor but innovative.

CHANGES NATIONALLY

Changes were on the way each year. Federal laws began under the leadership of Lyndon Baines Johnson. The 1969 Civil Rights Act included Title VI, still cited in suits against local school districts in non-compliance. The Bilingual Education Act was the start of a push towards educational equity and the acceptance of this Act as Title VII in the Elementary and Secondary Education Act was the boost needed to form coherent programs for English language learners. In 1970, Lau vs. Nichols was brought before the Supreme Court on behalf of San Francisco's Chinese speaking students. Justice Douglas wrote: "There is no equality of treatment merely by providing students with the same facilities, textbooks and curriculum; for students who do not understand English are effectively foreclosed from any meaningful education."

The '70's seem many life times past but their influence carries into the 21st century. The USA was at war in Vietnam until 1975. Vice President Rockefeller declared the CIA exhibited no signs of illegal activities, Microsoft became a registered trade name and Kodak invented the digital camera. The DOW closed that year at 858. The unemployment rate was 9.2%, a fact recognized by President Ford as a recession. An average home cost $39,300 and an average rental cost was $200 a month. In the 1970 census, no Hispanics were reported as homeowners in Willimantic. Do the economic indicators today show progress? There are still many children living in poverty and many more attending schools that do not offer full opportunity to all. The Windham Public Schools, under the guidelines of No Child Left Behind, must offer alternative schools to parents. No neighboring towns have accepted the letters from Windham administration requesting placement in their schools to children from Windham Schools where adequate yearly progress is lacking.

The Civil Rights Act and the resulting changes to the education of English language learners began a consistent growth in answering the questions related to minority language children. Title VII opened the minds of educators to special needs that were not learning disabilities in the traditional sense. District educators concerned for the fairness of offering equal opportunity to all children had the chance to propose programs that became models for other districts. Universities began to collect data and to publish results that would provide a background for classroom practices. Grants to programs and for research provided the base of models and data to the field of second language learning.

For those working with English Language learners (ELLs), the issue was always academic achievement. In the '70's and still in the Federal Register, the term for ELLs is Limited English Proficient (LEP). Researchers often prefaced their remarks by sincerely apologizing for the use of LEP a designation too close to leper. They wanted funding and they used the official terminology.

Being there at the beginning was a remarkable opportunity. There was scant research and no teacher training at the Universities to prepare teachers for English language learners. It is still rare today for the teachers receiving certificates to teach to have State required instruction in the needs, techniques and assessments that would be beneficial to second language learners. And in the '70's you can add the drawbacks of the field the absence of materials, books or technology that would support efforts in their classrooms. At a TESOL (Teachers of English to Speakers Of Other Languages) in Boston in 2010, a huge Convention Center was filled with materials for all languages, software, videos and support groups, all designed to raise the achievement of English language learners.

ESL At Sweeney Elementary School

The position at Sweeney Elementary School included grades K-5 and again, it was a pullout program for English language learners. Sweeney had been a middle school but a new high school released the former high school for use as a middle school. This switch gave children in the district that included the West Avenue housing project a school with room. Programs were added, including a Bilingual Program.

Sweeney School is located in a residential neighborhood. It sits near the top of a hill, parking lot to the left. The fields behind the school are now gone. The new Windham Middle School looks down on Sweeney from the top of the hill.

Inside, the one-story building spreads out to the right and left. The office is on the left and directly across from the front door is the combined cafeteria/auditorium. The Kindergarten, first and second graders turn right on entering, all others go to the left. It is a school that gives good vibrations, along with the smell of spoiled milk, and, in those days, chalk dust. Only two principals have been in residence since the day I started there. This must be a record and it speaks to the ownership teachers and administrators feel. A new principal started at the same time I did.

My job description was as vague as the state's policy towards English language learners. There wasn't an available room so my classes met inside the mainstream teachers' classrooms for grades K-1.

The youngest students needed to follow the mainstream instruction with extra time and repetition. It was quickly noticed that nursery rhymes were incomprehensible. Trying to explain them was an exercise in frustration. Although I didn't have access to Google at the time, I found a book that described Ring Around the Rosy as a reference to the Black plague. This was not too helpful. Other rhymes had words that we could work with through pictures. Mary's garden was intelligible if not relevant. I decided to move on to games to build vocabulary. The response was heart-warming, and noisy. We were definitely disrupting the rest of the class who were dutifully saying the letters and sounds of the alphabet.

My Spanish speakers were confident. Those who did not understand them were ignored. English talk was surely not directed at them so they spoke over it, around it and through it, creating pockets of noise in a class quietly becoming ready for learning. "Animals" a teacher said softly, and then showed her own amazement at what she had said. There was an attitude that the children should be grateful to be in this mainland school and that they should show their gratitude through respect and restraint. The children's understanding of this expectation was missing and they continued to have as good a time as possible.

I met with each group of mainstreamed children for an hour a day. Some of their Spanish-speaking peers went straight to the bilingual program. All those whose home language was Spanish were tested for English proficiency but parents made the final choice of program if there was a question of dominance. Those on the cusp of English proficiency had a hard road to walk, they started every day with good will that evaporated as the English continued and became more complex. ESL was their supplement but it wasn't enough. My own experience with five-year-old children revolved around building self-confidence and enjoying school. You can be sure that was not enough.

The difference in mainstream and bilingual program classrooms for the youngest children was remarkable. The best teachers I met over twenty-five years in Windham were at Sweeney that year and for many years to come. Noemi Alers, Rosa Tirado and Lydia Aponte were a trio of master teachers who brought strong ideas and stronger ideals to the new program. Their classrooms were orderly, warm and instructionally sound. It wasn't just language, it was the relationship with parents and the community that made them so effective. In those classrooms, the children belonged.

The "littles" were never my strength. I thought they were small miracles but couldn't imagine disciplining a child that still had dimples on his or her hands. The teachers who did manage well have all my respect.

The older children at Sweeney were moving along although the gap educators agonized over as the years went by was evident by 4th grade. And there was a constant stream of newcomers. On a walk through one day I looked in a classroom and saw a puddle of black hair covering a desk. It was a little girl, sitting alone at the back of the room. I tapped at the door and was waved in. The teacher said in a low voice, "she doesn't speak English". Continuing on she added, "this is an American School and I expect my students to speak English!" The lowered voice immediately caught the attention of her class and each student turned to look at Carmela. Again, with some reservations, it was not the teacher's fault. The school had offered no teacher support, no professional development to address the problem, no materials in either ESL or Spanish. In fact, there were few materials available. Carmela came in the midst of the school year with only a beginning knowledge of English and some gaps in her education in Spanish. I welcomed her to my 3rd grade hour and she began to speak in English in Sweeney School. I worried about her through her high school years and beyond. Her life was never easy but for good or for bad, she learned to be part of the mainland culture. The last time I spoke to Carmela she was just leaving her karate class.

Newcomers joined the classroom throughout the school year. They all needed vocabulary. There was no room for the class but the weather was a beautiful as fall in New England could be. It was time to go outside the box. Once upon a time I thought botany might be my calling and plants were still of interest. On the copse behind the school there was a trail made by the feet of those taking the back way to school.

Six students followed me onto the trail one sunny day. We moved in the shade of the trees, ready for anything new, dead or alive. We found quartz, fools' gold and the remnants of summer greenery. Flipping over rocks exposed insects settling in for winter. It was a liberating hour and we were late coming back to school. Each student left with a note explaining where he or she had been. Teachers graciously accepted them into their rooms. When I left school that Friday I felt we had found a true hands-on activity. Fridays in the woods were special treasure hunting days, full of things that grew, crawled or scurried. We identified things growing, moving, lying and dying in the square block of forest behind the school. Changes were recorded each week as the season progressed. Our leaf identification project was a many splendored collection of plastic baggies.

Shortly after our project became established, my class size dipped to two students. Did our fresh air fetish run out of fuel? No one knew what had caused an attendance problem directly related to ESL. We found out soon enough that five children were home bound with massive cases of poison ivy. We crossed the forest off our list.

Fridays it was still possible to go outside but we stayed on the black top part of the playground. Luckily there was as profusion of ants almost as many colored as the leaves. We introduced red ants to black ants, large ants to small ants, plotted their building sites and named them as tribes. Their food preferences were recorded in bound and dated notebooks with all other information. Our group was soon joined by whatever classes had come out side for a break. Our reputation as an interesting group grew.

The principal was observing ESL closely, in part because of the recent poison ivy scare. He noticed the growing popularity of our seven fourth grade students and decided to capitalize on the phenomenon.

The principal's decision to expand ESL to other children not quite up to the demands of the traditional classrooms resulted in the location of a Resource Room. For one hour a week, teachers could send down their behaviorally challenged students for reward time with my English language learners. This was beyond my wildest imaginings but it was a test of my skills and integration in general. It was now winter and we were inside.

Chess entered the resource room. The romance of knights, kings and queens involved history, vocabulary and a strong competitive spirit. Those that liked the game lived for Friday. A local high school student who lived across from Sweeney volunteered to come after his school hours to challenge the younger players. Beating Doug was the goal of many. Doug came in a wheel chair. This made no difference in their feeling that he was the god of the chessboard. No video games then, just checkers, dominoes, Chinese checkers and Old Maid.

The games were one project; cooking was another. We all learned measurements including the abbreviations for tsp. and tbsp. Ingredients built vocabulary as well although some of our recipes did not translate. Our first venture was tostones. A mother mentored this project, providing the ingredients and a tostone press. I brought a deep fryer. The tostones were delicious but the blackboard behind the table set up for cooking became speckled with flying droplets of hot oil. For years I went back to that school to face the mottled blackboard until the district replaced all blackboards and chalk with white boards and markers.

When spring came, our fame extended to the playground where my students proved to be the fiercest dodge ball players in the building. The very best were Enrique and Nancy, pushing each other to throw harder and quicker. They feared no one but everyone feared them. I understand that dodge ball has been discontinued in many schools. Maybe with reason.

Resource demanded intensive preparation and many props. The number and attitude of each new arrival couldn't be predicted so a number of projects to hand were all-important. Had I been more experienced, better trained, mentored or provided with materials for a particular group it might have been smoother. But it was positive and it was integration.

The joys of Resource were one hour a week. Classes for ESL were scheduled five days a week with forty minutes to an hour a day for each grade level. As I was able to pick up curriculum from the mainstream teachers it was easier to plan lessons around the vocabulary and concepts they were not mastering in the mainstream. Even those who started well in September were flagging by January. The sheer onslaught of English finally wore them down. The students were cooperative and we did well together but they learned ways to subvert the structure. I opened myself to one way when I noticed a bird on our windowsill one cold day. We discussed the bird and its error in staying in New England for the winter. Did the bird want to join our class? Should we encourage this? We did a lot of talking, and as the bell rang, one student mentioned that we hadn't done much work. I stupidly answered that there always had to be time "for the bird in the window" and I explained this as special opportunities that just pop up. The number of "bird" moments was astronomical for the rest of the year.

Part of the job was to visit families. Most of my students lived in the housing projects around West Avenue. It was a pleasure to see their families, to greet new babies and to know where my students were after school hours.

School always began well for English learners. September was a month for routines to be set and labeling was in the future. By October, robins and grackles were determined for reading groups. Cumulative learning was required. Most of the children just said no to the barrage of information, all of it in English.

THE SWEENEY
ELEMENTARY SCHOOL
BILINGUAL PROGRAM

Mainstream kindergartners and English language learners were compared every day. When a bilingual program teacher quietly said "permiso" in her classroom, all students were quiet and attentive. By the second week of school, a routine was established for entry and exit from the room, putting away materials and listening and speaking time. The children were respectful of each other and anyone else in the room. The two classrooms starting the kindergarten program were in charge of a new teacher from Puerto Rico who worked well with the children and bonded with the parents. The boys and girls sang the songs from the Island and parents were happy to join them at special events. De Colores is a favorite of mine and it is still sung. There were no discipline problems in these classrooms, and there was a great deal of learning. In short order, parents were asking to have their children retested for English proficiency in order to change to the bilingual program.

The new Puerto Rican teachers brought culture into the Windham Public Schools along with comprehensible instruction. Holidays and traditions from the Island became part of the school year, especially at Sweeney School. El Día De Los Tres Reyes is a traditional holiday in many countries. For years the Ukranian Church had celebrated in Willimantic but the growing Latino community was ready to institutionalize Epiphany in the schools. The Windham Board of Education felt, like Chanukah, Three King's Day was a holiday best left to home observance. This was not acceptable to the teachers.

THE THREE KINGS

Preparation for Three King's Day began in Sweeney in early November. The school supported twelve bilingual program classrooms, two for each grade, K-5. Grade level teachers were paired: one English speaking and one Spanish speaking. They all worked together on the preparations.

The community was also involved. Every Spanish speaker in the district volunteered. Three credible Kings were recruited. No camels at this first event but organizers were already thinking ahead. Gifts, food and music were listed as required pieces of the whole celebration. The first observance was held at Noble School because of its stage and seating. A professional artist from the community painted backdrops for the tableaus and presentations by the children. The number of people involved could not be counted, mostly because Fire Laws would kick in to block the doorways. The entire audience sang the songs of Navidad with the children.

Time off task was an issue at the schools. January 6th, by all that is holy, is the day of celebration. It could not be relied on to be a Saturday or Sunday. When administrators objected to the time taken for practice, the focus of preparation fell to the community. The next year's event was a shadow of the first. In town, the Puerto Rican Organization for the People (PROP) decided to take charge. Attendance for the event was high; attendance by Latinos in school was very low. Community activists brought the issue to the Board of Education. When administrators push for parent involvement they need to consider the results of their efforts.

Cities like Hartford and New Haven designated January 6th a religious holiday. It took many years for Windham's Board to agree to this policy. The initial effort allowed children to stay home with the district's blessing. It took almost 15 years for Epiphany to be a legal holiday on the school calendar. As the number of Spanish speakers rose from 9% in the '70's to almost 50% by the turn of the century, the overwhelming conclusion was to honor the community served by the schools. The whole community began to accept the change of the culture.

PROP was a victim of state and local budget woes. Today Three King's Day is celebrated with the help of Colectivo Mestizal, a group of local people dedicated to preserving the culture and traditions of Latinos. The traditions of Mexico have expanded the celebration and enriched it. The high school cafeteria filled the need for a time, stilt walking Kings rode puppet camels, gifts were in abundance and food was plentiful. Local politicians spoke and were translated into Spanish and best of all, the dance troop from Windham Middle School performed typical and current Latin dance. The Principal of Windham Middle School, Madeline Negron led the dancers.

Even the high school became too small. In 2009 the celebration was held at Eastern Connecticut State University, located in Willimantic. The merging of Town and Gown came under the wing of ECSU President, Dr. Elsa Nuñez.

The early concentration on keeping traditions alive was important because it brought the Latino community into the schools. Sweeney was definitely a comfort school. Although the principal did not supervise teachers in the bilingual program, he was sympathetic to their approach to education. The children were model students and they were learning. They were learning in the language they brought to school and they were soon readers. Math was also taught in Spanish and they learned the basic skills with ease. Their progress into the mainstream didn't begin until third grade at the earliest; many of the children took the Language Assessment tests and remained in the program.

KINDERGARTEN GRADUATION

Kindergarten Graduation was another major event, new to the mainland Kindergartens. If Three Kings' Day marked the winter semester, Graduation dominated the second. Robes were ordered with mortarboards, certificates and awards were prepared. And it was another opportunity to showcase the talent of the smallest students. The first graduation was a small event. The second was a production. The first filled an hour, the second lasted almost four hours.

It was patterned on Disney and the costumes were worthy of Disneyland. Every graduate had a costume, sometimes two. Each outfit was a replica a current Disney character and they were better than Hollywood's version.

On Graduation Day, parents arrived in groups until the cafeteria tables were filled. The food they brought was collected in the school kitchen for the feast to come. When it was time to start, a sigh passed through the room like a sea breeze floating across the beaches of the Island. The music was not quite strong enough to block the sounds of some forty excited five and six year olds lining up in the hallway.

The children entered from the back door of the cafeteria and paraded through the tables packed with parents and well wishers. Their seats were at the front, facing the stage. Their pace was somewhat ragged, impeded by masks and headpieces, other problems were minor. Mickey refused to hold hands with Minnie. Some left the parade to greet their parents. Other raced through, anxious to find their seats. At the same time the parade was going on in the cafeteria/auditorium, our peerless teacher was completing more costumes in the classroom. During the course of the program, many hands helped switch costumes so that it was difficult to remember which child belonged to which parent.

When the parade ended, it was time for awards. No child lacked a commendation. It took an hour to read each one and then diplomas were distributed. Every name was read in full, the student came front and center for a handshake, a kiss and a diploma. It was a solemn occasion.

Parents who had elected to go mainstream attended to watch their friends' and neighbors' children. It was the moment that reversed the tide towards mainstream placement. It became rare for eligible parents to choose mainstream classrooms.

The principal and teachers looked in from time to time with expressionless faces. The room used for the activities was directly across from the main entrance and the principal's office. A wing left led to the upper grades, the right hand wing was home to grades K-2. The assembling of parade participants and costume changers filled the corridor from the first grade drinking fountain to the upper grade bathrooms. The Teachers' Lounge was invisible. Mainstream children ate a bag lunch at their desks that day, smelling the odors of Island food that filled the building.

This was the end of Graduation in the school. The next year, kindergarten graduation moved to a local church. While there was no parade, the awards, presentations and student talent were all there. A parent committee selected the caps and gowns: navy for the boys and pink for the girls. Under the gowns were elaborate dresses or well-cut suits. The church tradition lasted for a few years but slowly died. One year it was decided to end it all and the children moved on to first grade like all kindergartners in the district. Graduation was re-named "Moving up day" but the memory of those early ceremonies will not end for several generations more.

Graduation marked the coming of summer and the end of the school year. I was called to Central Office for a change of assignment. The superintendent spoke in glowing terms of the joys of teaching in middle school.

Numbers in the middle school were increasing and a new team of two Spanish-speaking teachers for content subjects was the model. I would be the ESL teacher. In honesty, I knew kindergarten was not my best placement. Perhaps middle school would be a more appropriate position.

KRAMER MIDDLE SCHOOL

In the mid '70's the middle school was in the old high school building as the elementary school I left had been before the new high school was built. It was a Gothic building inside and out. Imposing, majestic, and full of hidden rooms, stairwells and accessible rooftops, this school was an architectural as well as educational challenge. The windows were huge and every gust of wind penetrated their edges. In summer, they effectively blocked the air as no one in their right mind would try to open those mammoth fixtures.

The first ESL room was an extension of the art room. It was completely isolated from the rest of the school except by going through the art room. While it was an admirable effort to contain the expected disruption, it made art a dicey class for the hundreds of students scheduled over the course of the week. This didn't work well and the ESL students were moved to a second floor classroom with many windows and easy accessibility for students, teacher and administrators. All program students were in

ESL class for two periods of English a day. Things went well for the first two months of the year.

My students were English language learners but in many cases they needed to grow in Spanish as well. They often had moved enough to disrupt their education and language development. Their new teachers brought high standards and a determination to teach every student.

There were few books and no budget that first year. Early on, one student, conscious of our needs, brought a box of new geography books into class. He said, "The Principal sent these to you." I should have thought this over but it was a delightful surprise. When the Principal finally located the books in our room, they were returned to their rightful owner.

We used the library and found some basic grammar books for reference. As the budget was readjusted we added fiction and non-fiction. A winner was anything the students found interesting.

The middle school included grades 6-8. All students were offered equal opportunity to make mistakes, assert rights and challenge the system. For non-English speakers, all problems were compounded. I noticed that my students seemed, in appearance, much older than the mainstream middle schoolers. The girls were beautiful and most of the boys seemed ready for the work force. Inside they were adolescents with all the angst of their age.

Carlos was in love with Raquelita. One day he brought a gun to school. I am not sure who was the target. It was the first and only time I assaulted a child but a quick kick allowed me to retrieve the gun. Others had fled for help. Our Vice-Principal, an ex-Marine, was not usually worried by bad behavior in the middle school. When he entered, the classroom was in some kind of shocked order. He found nothing to excite a reaction and asked if I wanted to report the incident. I did. It was over as quickly as it began and we all missed Carlos during his suspension. Soon after, Raquelita returned to the Island, and a few years later we learned she had died in an accident. Carlos finished school and became a local businessman, well respected in the community for sense and sensibility.

By holiday break, a routine was in place. Students were learning English although Spanish was the preferred method of communication. Family rivalries in the community spilled over into the classroom, marked by outbreaks of verbal and physical violence. Disagreements were labeled "business" and it was nothing the school could handle. At times students disappeared – they were sent to stay with family or friends in other cities until tempers cooled.

The status of ESL and the Spanish classes was low on the pecking order. When Mr. Ortiz was unable to come to school, no substitutes were hired; all students came to ESL for my classes and his as well. This became an on-going problem as too many students were spending too much time in close contact. A few rousing fights took place but soon "business" problems were settled after school hours. Our first teacher left and was replaced by a new Puerto Rican math teacher who managed to set up a perfectly disciplined classroom in less than a week.

After the holidays, students trickled in from vacations on the Island and some new students appeared as well. In the first class of the day in early January, four new boys, graduated in size, were seated in a row. They belonged to the same family and ranged in age from 12 to 19. Through the records they brought we determined that they were all in the same grade. And so they were assigned to the beginning ESL class and the schedule for content classes as they fit. Each day, in English, the youngest asked, "the letters, Missy?" Parents only receive Aid to Families With Dependent Children (AFDC) money for those children attending school. An official letter from the Principal of Kramer Middle School was needed to give the family eligibility. Four letters were to be written and they soon went home with the boys.

The oldest seemed the most out of place. He did not talk. At all. It took some time to realize that his teeth were black and broken. He was in pain. Only one dentist in town served those without insurance or funds. We went to see him after school and made an appointment for the next week. When he came back to school after the appointment he had no teeth at all. It took a few weeks to establish the need for teeth and finally, the dentist came through with that part of the job. My oldest student was now able to function without our help and he disappeared from the classroom. Blessings went with him; he did the best he could to survive.

There were three siblings left. Later one of them told me that the family had come to Willimantic for several reasons. First, there was a problem with the law best handled from a distance. There was also the coming need for a "caja". I wondered what that could be. Why would they need a box? A colleague from the Island translated the word into coffin. The second oldest son was not expected to live a long life. But he did. All three remaining boys followed me to the high school and so for many years

I was able to watch them as they adapted and became bilingual.

This was the year Kramer Middle School and, in fact, the whole district, addressed the issue of age and grade. It became a rule that anyone over 15 years went on to high school regardless of education completed. You can imagine the effect of this on the high school teachers and administrators. It was during the next year that the high school was added to my schedule for ESL services. Many of my ESL students appeared in classes at Windham High School. It certainly gave me the impression that we were family.

Perhaps independence was a better goal. There were students and parents who wanted no part of the bilingual program and they had the power to remove their children. The boys and girls placed in the mainstream did receive additional support and some were able to make the transition. Some were among the 9th grade students who were sophomores only because of the time spent in Windham High. By the time they reached 10h grade it was clear they would not graduate on schedule.

One student who entered Windham Middle School in 7th grade.quickly decided on a course of action and moved into mainstream classes. By high school, she was the undisputed leader. After completing University, Madeline Ramos returned as Assistant Principal of the new Windham Middle School. She drove in her Mercedes and was asked, "How did you get that car, Missy?" She replied, "I got an education." Madeline Negron is now Principal of Windham Middle School.

When the public expects each grade to learn faster and better than the one before, it is difficult to explain why there is not an orderly progression. Boards of Education don't recognize the differences in cohorts. One student can raise test scores to grade level; another student can lower them to show a serious gap. Looking to individual progress is the best way to measure teacher effectiveness and computers now help do this.

WINDHAM HIGH SCHOOL

As the 1980's approached, new laws such as Casteneda vs. Pickard sent the message that over emphasis on the development of English language skills is done to the detriment of a child's cognitive development and districts must take "appropriate action" to assure both educational concerns are addressed. This legal ruling is still pertinent as states vote in English Only mandates with ESL as the only intervention for English language learners.

Connecticut Public Act 77-588, effective November 1, 1977, required bilingual education if twenty or more speakers of a language other than English were in the same building. You may notice the loophole. Some districts moved the students from school to school to ensure that no one school would have more than twenty ELLs. Nevertheless, districts were mandated to determine English proficiency by testing and to document this process and its results. In 1979, the Windham Public Schools were 11% Hispanic (state terminology). Of this number, only a small group tested in need of bilingual education. Windham took this seriously.

A Spanish-speaking Sister at St. Joseph's church was totally opposed to the idea of bilingual education. As her church had a Spanish-speaking priest, she saw all Spanish speakers who were Catholic at some point, either on Sundays or at some major event. "Why are these young adults still in bilingual education programs?" Her question was a surprise and I told her that they had arrived in town last week, last month, last year and needed to keep learning. They were our newcomers, stretching resources to the limits. Evaluators are careful to define studies of English learners by time in program. Outsiders see only young adults who should have learned English in kindergarten.

At the high school, newcomers with minimal English were integrated and "treated just the same" as every other student. For those students who had been on the honor role in their former homes, this was horrendous. For the first time, many felt a lack of competence and a reluctance to speak in class. Teachers stressed that all students were graded, in part, on classroom participation. The newcomers resolutely kept their thoughts to themselves and took lower grades.

The bilingual program at the high school was asked to solve the problem of four young men who were determined to graduate despite the obstacles. They spoke English but were far behind in credits as they learned the language of school. It became clear that they would not drop out and were in for the long haul. Something had to happen. Pedro, David, Angel and Alejandro were close to graduating. The biggest problem was mandatory credits in English. The second biggest problem was the lack of support for them to meet the requirements of the English department.

Their class was one of my five scheduled ESL classes. Their records required a close look at requirements and credits in the bank. If our ESL classes could bump up to match the offerings of the mainstream there was a chance that ESL would be counted as a credit course. To the observer, they appeared fully fluent and so, once again, the blame was not the school's but the students'.

The English Department's solution for the new ESL classes was simple. There were Basic English books used for the Special Education students that would be a fit. I started my classes with studies of basic grammar, synonyms, antonyms, homophones, and irregular verbs. It was so boring to me and to the students that I went to the Head Teacher of the English Department with a well-planned plea. Finally, I was given a key to the English Department storeroom. What a joy! No budget, but lots of books. We started with an abridged Frankenstein. By beginning with discussion and expectations (most had seen the movie), we were able to get into a meaningful reading of a complete story. Did the citizenry misunderstand Frankenstein's monster? He was suspicious because he was different. All sympathies were with him.

The next trip to the storeroom turned up a full set of an American Literature anthology, discarded in favor of a new and shiny text. And so we began with the sermons of Cotton Mather. It was a perfect introduction to colonial America; and the sermons held as many morals as colonial primers. We talked of comparative religion, religion in the past and present, and religion on the Island and in Willimantic. Not one student lacked an opinion or the determination to express it. Students belonged to many religions, some were Catholic but many more belonged to the Pentacostal churches springing up in storefronts around Willimantic.

From religion we moved on to shelter for the body instead of the soul. Walden was not a good choice, but the next offering by Thoreau was To Build a House. This essay was the first real breakthrough. We built our own houses, pricing and comparing the good, the bad, and the ugly in local housing. One of our best conversations in English was on the definition of house and home. In Puerto Rico homeowners were not as rare as on the mainland. The number of Latino families who owned a home in Willimantic was miniscule in the '70's but the census of the '90's showed a growing number of owners. Some were my former students. Still, the idea of renting is strong. Windham Heights and West Avenue do not lack occupants and the projects are home to newcomers and long-term residents.

The readings in the book were not all winners and we selected readings together. Once chosen, we read through each a piece. Complete with discussion of merits and shortcomings. Somewhere in the midst of the anthology I decided to match periods of American history with literature. And so we read Across Five Aprils, The Witch of Blackbird Pond, Sounder, and Travels with Charlie. I had to discard Sounder for emotional reasons. It made me cry, and then everyone cried. We left the room looking like refugees from the great flood.

One special story was Jack London's To Light a Fire. Reading this on a cold winter day in Connecticut brought waves of nostalgia to recent arrivals who expected

Connecticut to test their survival skills. Which is worse? Extreme heat or extreme cold? Maybe extreme anything was the decision of the class.

Mainstream classes read most of the books chosen. In ESL a little more time was spent relating history with literature and filling in background for periods and places. This was the most challenging part of my teaching career. I came to believe that my ESL students did not need easy readers; they needed to read whatever their peers were reading, and they needed to catch up on the parts of the culture their peers had internalized in past years. At the end of our literature semester, one very bright young man noted, "I never thought I'd read literature." But he did, and with a perspective that was fresh.

At a conference for teachers of ELLs, an Assistant Superintendent in Hartford made fun of a teacher who was working with her class on Shakespeare! The administrator made clear the stupidity of her decision. To me, his stupidity was more than equal to any I'd experienced yet. Of course they should hear the stories of Shakespeare. They just needed a bit of background and a lot of patience to understand it. The universal themes in Shakespeare were as fully understandable as West Side Story.

Most of the students felt able to enroll in a mainstream English class the next school year. A very sympathetic English teacher, who later became a missionary, offered to enroll them as a group in her class on American folklore. This sounded so right.

The first week is surely the hardest, I thought with apprehension. The second week escalated student panic. And by the third week it was time for a conference with the teacher. American folklore sounds like fun but it is the equivalent of learning thirty nuanced words for coffee bush in Spanish. Shakespeare was easy compared to Huckleberry Finn.

Students were first introduced to Paul Bunyan. Then came Pecos Pete. The characters spoke in the vernacular of their part of the United States with "y'alls" and other incomprehensible English. And Huckleberry Finn was next. The opening test was a nightmare that left the teacher aghast. How could such simple stories produce so much confusion? The next assignment was to write an essay on a favorite bit of American folklore. Our ESL classroom problem was to decide if Puerto Rican folklore counted. Several of the students felt that Juan Bobo stories should qualify and so began translating them. Juan had not crossed the water to join Paul Bunyan in the folkloric tradition of heroic behavior. He was a classic bobo. Not the best metaphor to compete with America's legendary heroes.

It was decided that perhaps another class would be a better entry vehicle. The students were placed in Basic English, filling out workbooks heavy on grammar and irregular verbs.

The ESL students came from the bilingual program as true beginners, from the mainstream as lacking English credits, and from Spanish-speaking countries at any time during the school year.

The first bilingual program at the high school was entrusted to three teachers. Two were Spanish speakers, responsible for science, math, social science, and Spanish literature. The third held the charge for English. This worked out to six classes daily for each teacher with one period left over for planning. The ESL teacher taught 5 classes daily, adjusting to the level of English. As content subjects were designed for grade level, the English classes were a mix of ability, age and grade. At this early stage, ESL was not considered an alternative to a mainstream English class, but it became evident that without accepting ESL for an English credit there would be a long wait until graduation.

The ESL classroom had 12 tightly packed desks. There were 15 to 20 students as the year progressed. We were close in every sense of the word. The room was 230B, almost like the train track entrance leading to Hogwarts. It had been the social studies department storeroom until they outgrew it. There were lots of shelves for books filling one wall, and a window across the back of the room. Under the window the radiator offered extra seating for overflow crowds.

One morning, I walked in to find graffiti, torn paper, and upended bookcases in the room. SPIC LOVER was inoffensive, but other epithets written in poster paint across the blackboard and walls weren't as pleasant. This was the worst incident in a series of subtle events.

I started down to the principal's office, seeking justice, support and maybe a new room with a lock. It took awhile to find him and convince him to accompany me to 230B, but he did.

When we arrived and opened the door, the room was neat with only a blush of red on the walls. All my students were sitting expectantly at their desks ready for the day to begin. It looked like a model classroom.

The Students

My students were tactful. As I walked down the hall with one of my new arrivals, he suddenly said, "You really like that green suit, don't you?" I had never thought about it much, but it didn't wrinkle and it fit so I guess I wore it often. Looking at it closely I understood that it was time to retire the suit. My students dressed well. They looked good. I added a sun streak to my hair, my son told me I looked like road kill; my students said I looked younger. Being young was important.

The average age of our Hispanic citizens was considerably lower than the rest of the population. My fellow teachers brought in a birthday cake on my 43rd birthday. Students switched the numbers to read 34. They were embarrassed by my great age and so I became 9 years younger.

In late fall, yearbook pictures are taken, an important time. My students were going to graduate. In these early months my only unbreakable rule was not to cut my class. One day, two were absent. I was really fussing and couldn't let it drop, so the next day when they returned they had a lecture on promises and responsibilities. No one said a word. When class was dismissed one of the other boys stayed behind to explain the absence. It seemed that Pedro didn't have a jacket for the picture, so Alejandro walked home and got him one. Home was Windham Heights, a good four mile walk one way on a rainy November day.

When Jose came to Windham in the second grade, he was diagnosed Learning Disabled. The LD classroom was taught in English so he spoke Spanish at home and English at school. The 20 minutes we spent together in ESL did little to help. The year that testing was mandated for language dominance, it was determined that Jose was clearly Spanish dominant. He moved to the Bilingual Program and began learning to read in Spanish with additional reading classes in English. It took additional time to realize that language was not the problem; Jose was LD in his first language as well. Bilingual remedial staff was not funded then and each year a new approach was tried. He finally had a trained teacher located in the migratory staff. Despite his problems, Jose was excellent in mathematics and he had an incredible memory. His knowledge of current events was accurate and detailed. But his inability to write well in Spanish or English became a wall of frustration. In the mainstream, art and shop were his courses of choice. He participated in the wrestling team and in boxing. I hope to meet him again as he was the kindest of all the students I had and because he always called me "teacher". My failure to help him still rankles; he was well able to learn.

Arnaldo entered Windham High School at age 16 as a freshman. He had not attended school since 2nd grade. During the years out of school he contributed to the family in many ways but now he was to attend school. Luckily, we found a trained tutor in Spanish and Arnaldo's efforts to learn were outstanding. At a planning session, it was decided to concentrate on reading and writing in Spanish the first year, with vocabulary building in English. The second year would start reading in English and a Remedial Reading teacher added him to her list. For the four years at Windham he passed all requirements for graduation: content in Spanish and as much English as could be fit into the school day. He left Windham literate in his first language. His first job was at a local supermarket. When I heard "Arnaldo, pick up line 4" it brought a silent cheer.

The favorite words in Melvin's beginning English were "heavy duty" and "hanging around". Both said with a smile. He also came to Windham at age 16, a serious and well-educated young man. His dream was medical school. The first year he studied hard and made the school Honor Roll as part of the Bilingual Program. The second year he moved on to mainstream classes. He kept ESL on his schedule and was no longer on the Honor Roll. Each assignment took two or three times longer than it should have, but assignments were completed well. There weren't enough hours in the week to produce the essays, poems and story analyses required by his mainstream English teachers. In ESL we were reading The Red Badge of Courage. This small class had gotten into a heavy discussion of chivalry when the Vice Principal came in to observe. We continued to discuss the behavior of the characters and the nature of honor. Before the class closed, the Vice Principal asked Melvin if he would answer the question, "Why did you come here?" The bell rang and the question went unanswered. Melvin was, like all his peers, a citizen of the USA. Melvin did go to the University of Massachusetts, entering the same year as my youngest son. Early on they shared notes in Biology class. He fit in well with Latino students from the Boston area although they came with their own cliques and attitudes. He did graduate and went on to head one of the first community schools funded in Springfield through Title VII. He could answer the question posed by the Vice Principal now but it wouldn't be asked. I was fortunate enough to attend Melvin's 50th Birthday last fall. He lives in Florida, is working towards a PhD in environmental biology and teaching adults. His brothers are still in the area. All five had been in my classes and each one was and is special. Lem is still extremely energetic in a very positive way, Jerry a Fire Captain in my town, Harry an artist when he has time and Efren raising a family and doing well. The parents seem the same but the devotion of their children must be keeping them young.

Nancy and Enid came junior year with good educational backgrounds. They had ESL and perhaps one course in the bilingual program but the mainstream was their destination. Both girls were beautiful, both made friends quickly. The transition to an English speaking school was not easy but in two years they were ready for University work. Nancy came back to Windham as a teacher; Enid took her special education talents to Hartford and continued her studies for graduate degrees. Nancy is now a Facebook friend, teaching in Atlantic City. Enid is teaching in Hartford and I was lucky enough to see her recently. No one would guess they arrived in Connecticut without English now.

Carmela, my 5th grade new arrival at Sweeney Elementary, moved with me to Kramer Middle School and then to Windham High School. She was still below grade level in reading and as the official reading teacher was over-subscribed, Carmela worked on reading in the ESL room. We read books on nursing, her interest, phonics and vocabulary. If in doubt, Carmela reverted to Spanish pronunciations. The thinking of the time was to sound out a word and then grasp the meaning. The scrambled sounds didn't translate well into English words. She was learning spoken English quickly and at age 13 she enlisted at Windham Hospital as a candy striper. She had heavy responsibilities for her younger siblings at home, especially when her family was called back to the Island. I believe Carmela did more housework than I and she also continued her work at the hospital logging a record number of hours. But when the darkest days of winter were relieved only by the whiteness of the snow, Carmela left school. She came back to school briefly to show her rings: she had married.

Because they appeared older, many of the girls were dating adults, and many left school to pursue the dream of their own apartment, children, and independence from family rules. For every girl who left, another determined to do well academically, graduate, and continue to college. In those times, it was clear that more of the girls were motivated by books than the boys. In general, it was the boys who arrived late, with good academic backgrounds, who carried on after high school graduation. For the others something happened to them in the public schools that gave them reason to try other paths unrelated to education. It is hard to be macho when English-speaking teachers are not cooperating with the concept and it was critical to be macho in Windham.

It is impossible to try to explain how different each of the students were. They were not the "ESL students" but individuals. Even when a full family came to the school there was no way to predict their likes and dislikes, goals or behavior. In one exemplary family, the five boys reacted in completely opposite ways. The youngest had been on the mainland the longest, the three oldest came in high school. All have done well. It is notable that the oldest, who had the advantage of being educated on the Island in Spanish were the best students. They came with a very good education. Their home life had always been warm, loving and supportive of whatever plans they made. One is still working on a PhD. A second retired from the U.S. Army. Other families were harder to identify. The names were not the same but the family spirit always came through.

One corner on the second floor was the designated meeting place for the program students. It was near the Bilingual Program Office that also acted as a classroom, meeting place or testing area. Our storage space was there in the early years and it became a place to store student valuables as well. I did notice that only our students seemed to be in that part of the second floor. I was told later that it was not a place other students willingly walked by and there were other options to get from A to B. In some ways adversity gave us a bond. We had the poorest space as teachers, they had the smallest classrooms in the building. We eventually conquered by numbers.

FIELD TRIPS AND LOVE IN A COLD CLIMATE

Driving to work on a Monday morning was painful only because the day would be spent inside. The sky was vivid blue, the air crisp. Trees in the distance had the appearance of enormous flower gardens. Along the roadside were small woodland creatures in various stages of decomposition. It was fall in New England, not a day to ignore.

The best weather of the year had arrived. I remarked on the incredible cloud formations to my class. They responded with their favorite sky – one with bright sun and no clouds at all.

For two months we had studied The House of the Seven Gables, which we read in an abridged version, and currently, The Crucible in its entirety. This fall the ESL classes had found something of interest: curses, witchcraft, vengeance, and predators. The settings were different, but background knowledge worked well. We were reading together with concentrated effort to understand another time, another America, forgetting the political nuances in Miller's play. Whoever determined that high school students from other countries could only be interested in topics relevant to their personal lives was mistaken.

The culmination of all this hard work was a field trip to Salem, Massachusetts. Most ESL students did not go on the school- sanctioned field trips, partly because travel money went to departments, and ESL was not in one at that time. We finally convinced the principal that this was not quite right, and so now we were free to move about the country. Salem was the choice for fall, and we planned to visit the House of the Seven Gables, and the Museum of the Salem Witch Trials and to walk streets where real witches walked among us.

Permission slips came in on time, buses were booked, tickets pre-purchased, and bag lunches requested from the cafeteria. The day came. Lined up by the bus stop, in pairs, was the best-dressed, most orderly group of high school students ever to leave Windham High on a field trip. Each girl had a partner and each boy had his girl. The planning for this alone must have taken weeks. I felt under-dressed but thankful.

I hadn't convinced anyone else to join us as chaperones and the thoughts of unruly young men and terrified young ladies was daunting. However I found that this was an event taken seriously. One student asked quietly if he had brought enough money. He had thirty dollars, more than I did, but he was leaving town and had a reputation to uphold. I just had to bring them all back safely.

We were off. After about an hour, the bus driver turned to me and asked, "Do you know where we get off the highway?" I had no idea where we were and hoped we hadn't yet left the country. She called home office, got directions, and we arrived in Salem only slightly late for our appointed tours.

In town I was prepared with a map and timelines. Witches did walk the streets, not as tourist attractions but as part of their day. We found the Witch Museum and made our scheduled entry time. The characters from The Crucible stood on platforms above our heads. The programmed mannequins spoke lines from the play, lights were dim, and the feeling of knowing these people was real to us all. Not one of my students spoke: they listened to the programmed characters. They knew the words.

The walk to the House of the Seven Gables was another surprise. If there had been puddles my gentlemen would have laid their jackets over the muddy waters. Each couple found a bench, rock or step to sit on for lunch break. We toured the house, peered into the well and then walked down the promenade and looked out to sea.

The school had provided brown bag lunches. Benches became intimate dining rooms for two. There were not enough benches to spread out so couples found walls and steps to prepare for the meal together. It was a beautiful day for the end of October. The town was magic.

It was a remarkable first attempt at leaving "home" for me especially. I was determined to try again come spring. The results showed in classes - it no longer seemed that teachers had only boring tales to tell. And not too long after graduation, at least three of the couples on that trip married. That was never a prediction to be answered on the field trip application.

Many of our trips away from Windham involved the growing reputation of the dancers. We were invited to other schools and performed brilliantly. Break dancing was added to the routine and then popularity soared. Albie, Tony, Henry, Kenny, Donzelle, Todd and Tim composed as diverse a team as could be imagined. They were really good. The University of Connecticut paid the group to march and dance in the Homecoming parade route through campus. The first paid performance. They arrived and joined the marchers. Shortly after the parade started an irate upper classman, acting as "parade marshal" rushed at the boys and told them to leave. I had been walking along with them and, equally irate, told him they were being paid to participate. He was stunned but defeated. When we gathered to go home I looked at the break dancers. They were in bad shape – bloody hands, torn shirts and bruised heads. Break dancing is not so good on concrete. No one had complained or even mentioned the damage.

The schools continued to call for performances. I finally realized that there was never any interaction of students visited and students visiting. I asked the next teacher who called for a show about having the troop come early and perhaps have lunch with some of the students at the target school. There was a long silence. She answered that it was not built into the schedule. Clearly, they wanted to have performers to entertain but not to mingle. We stopped the visits then and restricted shows to more welcoming audiences.

The desire to leave and see new sights was always there. For those who had seen only Willimantic there was an undercurrent of jealousy towards those who had grown up in Puerto Rico, Mexico, Colombia or another exotic locale. Even New York City sounded romantic although those relocating in Willimantic found it a lot safer than Spanish Harlem. Willimantic was definitely a quiet place. There was a movie theater, now a Performing Arts Magnet School. A few restaurants, a five and ten and a fashionable men's clothing store were the big attractions. As the population grew, Latin restaurants and groceries opened, replacing the clam chowder and corn muffins of the early eating places. The change in town is more visible than in the schools, except for the triumph of the new technologically perfect Windham Middle School.

A Class of Our Own

After the holidays we returned to school. By mid-January it was cold enough to turn north-facing windows into prison bars. My cat tried each outside door that morning, expecting that if she chose the correct one she would enter into a world of warmth and butterflies. An icy drive down the hill to school came to a sliding end in time for bus duty. Then I noticed two of my newcomers scaling the mounds of plowed snow between the street and the sidewalks. They wore jeans, sneakers, and t-shirts. One had a bright smile; his brother seemed more realistic. His jaws were clenched, his face blue. They had arrived in New England after the holiday, Puerto Rico to Willimantic in four hours. Children of the Airbus who faced a change of climate, culture, clothes, and language in deepest winter with a smile. We drove to the nearest Thrift Store after school closed and found parkas and boots. My car door froze open and one brother held it tightly as we came back to town. Eventually one returned to the Island, the other stayed on to become a town Selectman, State

Commissioner and leader of all things Latino. He is a gift that keeps on giving.

As newcomers continued to arrive throughout the school year, the need for another room was clear. At first we "shared" rooms on a whoever-has- a- free- period basis. When a teacher on the second floor had planning time, for example, that room was free for ESL. I had strict orders from each teacher to touch nothing, to put up nothing on the walls, and to clean the blackboards thoroughly before leaving the room. I considered handcuffing each student to a desk. It was in these rooms that English language learners began to notice what was happening in the rest of the building.

Each day brought a complaint from someone who felt the room was had not been left as found. The complaints did not always come directly: a very good number of grievances went straight to the Principal. As numbers increased and students wandered the halls looking for whatever room we might be in at any given time, the Principal realized the seriousness of the situation, and a room was located and allocated to ESL. It was a corner room with a full complement of desks, windows, bookcases, screens, and map holders. Its walls were ours. The existence of this room gave hall monitors an easy direction for any non-English speaking roamers.

Now that we had space, it was possible to sign up for audio-visuals. Movies were ordered, and transparencies, records and tapes were added to instructional tools. Students became proficient in the use of the projector, the overhead, and screens. We had moved into the 20th century.

All teachers had hall duty between classes. The idea was to stop any problems in the four minutes allotted to move from room to room. There really were few issues so one teacher decided to patrol for the use of Spanish. As students passed her assigned spot, she would dart out, hissing, "speak English" if any deviation from the language of the USA was noted. As teachers from Puerto Rico came into the district her problem was compounded. These teachers spoke Spanish in the Teachers' Lounge, creating another small Island in the sea of English around them. A complaint was made to the Principal and to me. The idea of allowing this practice to continue bothered her until the day she retired.

Many of the teachers were more than willing to help with specific curriculum projects. A science teacher spent hours in one of my classes with a prepared hands-on lesson in radioactive materials. She brought a Geiger counter and the attentive behavior of the students convinced her that we could carry through with other projects throughout the year. A music teacher gave me his planning book so that we could study the vocabulary of music. I found new workbooks titled Content Across the Curriculum and we studied political science, economics and social studies with as many real life examples as I could find. It is not sure that these lessons provided insights into those subjects but we all learned the words to explain the concept of partisanship, depression and culture clash.

In the third year of the program, one Spanish-speaking teacher, Jose Aponte, became Director of Bilingual Education. These were good years. Students were exceptional and our Puerto Rican boys and girls were joined by three exchange students from Mexico, several from Colombia, and the brother of a local Doctor from Korea. These students fostered competition and English improved quickly. In one year, we accomplished every objective and decided we needed to raise expectations.

Moving Into The Mainstream

Baseball

Moving Into the Mainstream community came through the efforts of teachers, the sheer brass of students and the curiosity of those high school students in the mainstream. The program began a dance troupe under the direction of Luis Diaz and Victor Alers. Students practiced choral readings. They performed across the state and were in such great demand they were able to choose where to appear. We celebrated Cinco de Mayo with traditional foods made by Olga from Mexico with the help of her new Island friends. One exchange student from Mexico came from a wealthy family. He persisted in drawing pictures of his home featuring three garage doors. He was accepted, but just barely. The numbers and good feelings moved over him in waves. He had to change or be washed overboard.

Sports were a large part of Windham High spirit. A rule requiring that students must play on the Junior Varsity team before acceptance as Varsity rules militated against those late arrivals from the Island. Victor Alers, one of the Bilingual Program teachers, came from International University in San German with a degree in physical education and an ability to coach any high school student from girl's swimming to baseball. Moreover, all of the students respected his talent.

Through Victor, the baseball team opened to admit newcomers to Varsity. As coach he did more to integrate students than any program before or after. And the team was good. Victor arranged for the group to travel to Puerto Rico to play Island teams. Teams on the Island seem almost professional, in part because they can play throughout the year. Only private schools have teams, the others play in leagues. Relatives on the Island had the schedule in advance. Players were able to meet with family and friends during the tour. The only mishap was serious sunburn for a pale-faced Connecticut native.

Victor had permission from the Board of Education for the trip held during spring break, April 4th to 8th. Almost 30 boys were on the plane, from freshmen to Varsity. It was the first time they had played together as a team. Some were flying for the first time. There were many "firsts" on that trip.

Two games were scheduled with the Island teams and the rest of the time would be practice. Coach Alers had a firm conviction that every player would get the opportunity to play, even if it were just one inning.

1985
WINDHAM HIGH'S BASEBALL TEAM ON TOUR IN
PUERTO RICO WITH COACH VICTOR ALERS, COACH
CHRIS RISLEYAND CHAPERONES ALGIS BALINSKAS,
JEAN ROMANO AND JAN HUBER

WAITING FOR THE ISLAND'S TEAM

You may notice that the mother on the right was properly dressed for the event. I had worn a Windham T-shirt and slacks, the typical outfit in Connecticut.

The day was warm, the boys played brilliantly. Windham lost the game but the lasting impression was a win. During Coach Alers four years with the Varsity team, they won sectionals and played excellent teams around Connecticut.

That trip with Victor and his two assistant coaches bonded the team members and gave common memories to take home. Coach Alers said later that his main point was to show the mainstream athletes that Puerto Ricans were excellent baseball players and that the Island was special. He proved this in a four day trip.

EVERYTHING WAS OPEN

In those days, team sports for girls were not common. The Latinas were parade oriented and became exceptional majorettes. The two M's, Maribel and Magaly were joined by Liliana. They were perfect.One student from Colombia came without ever hearing English spoken. She tried out for the Drama Club with no fear and became Liat in South Pacific.

A new concept, X period, began once weekly to promote student interaction in a productive way.

Many students in Willimantic had duties or jobs after school hours; this time gave them a chance to participate in clubs or activities. My contribution was named International Club. I don't know what I expected but the club became a popular destination for students who had watched the delights of the Latin culture from the sidelines. Dance was the priority. All of the girls wanted to dance Latin style. Boys followed girls and the club grew.

Period X consumed much of my preparations on Wednesday evenings. The group had big ideas and one was a field trip together. To do this, we would need a fundraiser. I hate asking for money. Maybe two fund raisers. We planned a community wide International Fair with booths from every ethnic group in Willimantic. Food, artifacts, dance (we all learned to dance the Horah from Aida Nesselroth). None of us had an idea of the number of Ukranians, French, Lebanese, Polish, Irish, Israeli and Latino adults who were ready to party with high school students. Many hours were spent tracking down the ethnic clubs, churches and meeting halls of Willimantic. We made a bit of money. Second fund raiser – a dance with pop music and some Latin songs thrown in. The disc jockey, Tony Laboy, worked hard at keeping one eye on the music and one on his girlfriend. Our field trip was going to happen.

A bus was chartered for the trip to New York City. Our destination, by group vote, was the Statue of Liberty, a fitting choice for the International Club. It was also a choice acceptable to the administration that vetoed some of the original choices. Two members of the mainstream were best friends, one black, one white. They were wonderful kids and I can still see their faces, so honest so sincere! As we unloaded the bus near the ferry to Ellis Island, I saw the two quickly entering the subway. I never did see the Statue of Liberty that day. I waited by the subway entrance until they returned loaded with mementoes from Chinatown. The nimchuks were confiscated, the fireworks packed away but the memories went home with them.

A few years later the school developed a Race-Culture Committee to bring students together. It answered problems raised by teachers who were more than aware of racial tensions in the school. The all out effort was a response to NEASC's ten-year evaluation. Bert Phillips, President of Bermujltinational Limited operated a consulting firm located in Silver Springs, Maryland. His work in business and government included work with school climate. He coordinated the seminars and brought a sense of humor to a situation that could have been approached with too great a depth of gravitas. The program grew to offer retreats for both students and staff. There were discussions, role-playing and activities to build sensitivity. I am sure it helped but integration was moving steadily on regardless of staff input. Shortly before the Race-Culture seminars began, a very supportive English teacher brought me a list of concerns drawn up by teachers who had been observing the bilingual students and Latinos in general. Their concerns were real and their desire to help was clear. I thought about this and then brought it to Madeline, then a high school student. I asked her to think about the list and respond. Her response was to call a meeting of students in order to compose a second list that detailed their own concerns with observed teacher behaviors. We were moving along. Every opportunity produced a leader. The confidence level of the students rose every year.

GRADUATING

In 1967, only one Hispanic had graduated from Windham High; times were changing. Students and teachers planned a graduation party for theClass of '80 that celebrated their accomplishment Latin style. It was held at the Polish-American Club in Willimantic. There were 21 Latino graduates that year, and everyone had done well. That night they danced to Latin music, received awards, and posed for pictures. At school, the Awards Assembly was a tribute to the other students; no Hispanic received an award in those years, the competition was stacked against them because they were out of the mainstream. It was accepted as how things were in the early years and unquestioned. I asked to establish a special award for a Spanish-speaking student. The answer: "that would be discriminatory."

The graduation of the Class of 1980 was special, in part because of the students from Mexico and Colombia. The mix was magic. After classes, Lydia Aponte and students worked to create a theme a goal and decorations, programs and a dedication. One student wrote a poem for the class. It is included here to ensure her words will live on.

Despedida-Clase Graduande por Migdalia Bonilla

Compañeros, ya nos vamos
Volverémos a oparnos
En la sombra insospechada
De otros sender lejano?

Volveran las ilusiones
Y los corazones candidos,
Entre rimas y canciones
Lagrimas y desengaños?

Como tiernas mariposas
Por el mundo a volarvamos,
Con las alas son mojadas
Y los sueños esbozados.

Los sueños se han hecho versos,
Y los versos se haran brazos,
Que la vida será dura
Y el camino será largo
Mas, no importa, compañeros
Llevaremos a recaudo

El caudal de los recuerdos,
Y llevamos tanto y tanto!

Mañana, cuando volvamos
En un recodo a encontrarnos.
Viviremos el encanto
Del recuerdo emocionado.

Nuestras almas serán, nuevas
Nuestros cuerpos seran sanos
Porque el esfuerzo constante
No Habra reconquistado.

Hasta luego, companeros,
Volveremos a encontrarnos!

That class was special and others followed. The class of 1980, whose Latino students received no awards at assemblies, had eight students enroll and complete requirements for B.A. degrees. One continued on for a PhD in Educational Psychology, the student from Mexico became a lawyer and four came back to teach at Windham.

In the '80's the students moved towards the mainstream, giving up their own graduation for the school-wide Senior Night held at the Eastern Connecticut State University sports center. They had proven their ability to compete well and they were no longer separated, they were a part of the high school culture.

Something was lost in the transition to mainstream activities. There was no Latin music, no hectic planning of themes, colors and awards. Graduation Day was for the parents and students but the celebration followed the routine of mainstream culture.

Eastern Connecticut State University has a campus directly across the street from Windham High School. It almost seems an extension of Windham. Since the '80s, ECSU has grown and added buildings to house new programs. The new President, Elsa Nuñez, is part of the community as President David Carter was before her arrival. The University connection is important to the Windham Public Schools and the willingness to share has broadened the perspective of the school district.

Professional Development for Classroom Teachers of ESL

Conferences for bilingual program teachers were usually sponsored by OBEMLA, the Office of Bilingual Education and Minority Language Affairs in Washington, D.C. The conferences were held in places where practices might help those in the field. Albuquerque, Washington D.C., Tucson, San Francisco all had programs in place so that attendees could both learn from the master practitioners, or just from those struggling like us, or from observing bilingual programs in action.

TESOL, Teachers of English to Speakers of Other Languages, also had conferences in each state as well as nationally. In 1981, ConnTesol held its eleventh conference in Meriden, Connecticut. The keynote speaker was Mrs. Penelope Alatis, Chairperson on the ESL in Secondary Education Special Interest Group of TESOL International.

She addressed the ESL teachers' role beyond the classroom, assuming that all ESL teachers were adequately trained for instructional duties. Her first point was that the ESL teacher should act as guide for all the faculty, providing orientation on the background of ESL students and requesting information from content teachers on the needs of students in their classes. Mrs. Alatis' second point described the ESL teacher as a generalist, able to address information on all content areas. And third, Mrs. Alatis noted the value of the ESL teacher for the Guidance Department, assisting with student placement and especially watching out for inappropriate placements, for example, in special education classrooms. An important function was the use of the ESL teacher as a trainer and coordinator of volunteers, aides, supplementary services, nurses or other health officials. And most important, the ESL teachers should act as buffers between school and home.

The ESL teacher must be able to leap over tall buildings in a single bound. I found myself trying to relearn geometry, an awesome task. Second language learners were slated to the ESL classroom during their study periods for assistance with classwork, homework or lack of work. If another class was in progress help might not be forthcoming and the student would return to the mainsteam class with the news that enlightenment was tabled until another day. I don't think many teachers realized what was happening but they did feel ESL was ineffective. When Professional Development workshops given by the State Department of Education brought focus on the early research, it hardly answered the concerns faced in district ESL classes.

Although the analogy irritated me, a comparison between ESL and special education was made quite often. When I became an administrator, the head of Special Education told me we were really in the same business. I couldn't accept her statement and found it offensive. Both groups of identified children had special needs, that is true, but the teaching techniques, pace and goals were different for ESL. Another truth is closer to making the connection: the ESL teacher is expected to be master of all content, able to pick up any second language learner and find a way to guide the student through chemistry, American history or first grade phonics. In Connecticut, certification for ESL covers large grade levels, resulting in a need for large knowledge banks. The special education teacher is viewed in a similar manner as a teacher able to work miracles. Both educators need special training in assessment and while it has long been part of special education it was not in the ESL curriculum in the early days.

Remembering that this was in 1981 is difficult as the same concerns are true today. Recognition of the role of ESL teacher has not progressed as much as it could. Few other faculty in high schools see the ESL teacher as a valued asset and school administrators rarely invite ESL teachers to join in creating policy. Federal funding has helped increase the University role in providing professional development for in-service ESL teachers. I met one teacher in a graduate program at the University of Connecticut. This Windham teacher, in 2009, persisted until the administration who planned a new Academy setting for in-coming freshman founded a counterpart for English language learners. Many problems she faces are those noted almost 30 years ago; we need a strong push to empower exceptional teachers like Joan.

PART II:

ADMINISTRATION

The true test of civilization is not the census, nor the size of cities, not the crops, - no, but the kind of man the country turns out.

Ralph Waldo Emerson (1803-1882)
Essays: Society and Solitude.

LEAVING THE CLASSROOM

In 1985, Ronald Reagan took the oath for a second term as President of the United States of America. In October, terrorists hijack the Achille Lauro, an Italian cruise ship and in November, terrorists seize Egyptian Boeing 737 airline after its take-off from Athens. AIDS continues to spread, famine in Ethiopia and pop stars in America join in a fund raiser for those suffering in Africa and sing "We Are The World". The average cost of a house reached $89,330 with average monthly rent at $375. Hispanics made the US census as homeowners in Willimantic. A US Postage stamp cost .22 and a gallon of gas was $1.09. Windham was peacefully unaware of many of the events of the times; in fact, few American citizens realized portents that would bring terrorism, AIDS and high gasoline prices into their daily lives. At one of my first Central Office meetings, an Assistant Superintendent took a discussion of AIDs off the agenda as an issue that would never affect Windham.

My opportunity to move to Central Office as Director of the Bilingual Program came as the Director in place decided to open a business and change career paths. After ten years of teaching, there were many issues I hoped to challenge and the only way was through administration.

Leaving the classroom was difficult. The idea of looking at the whole sequence of ESL from pre-K to high-school graduation was awesome. I had touched base with some of the students I met in my first positions in the elementary schools and knew they could have moved faster, done better. Maybe we could lean on new research and optimism to ensure the next ELLs would reach full potential.

In the '70's, Willimantic's population was 16% Hispanic, in 2009 the term minority requires a definition. Is the minority measured by numbers in nation-wide, or is the minority only in the perception of the viewer? Over 30 years, the minority has become the majority in Windham's schools. The question is whether or not the shift has made life better for the Latino students. At issue is not bilingual education in any of its many forms; it is how to promote equal opportunity.

When I moved to Central Office as Director of Bilingual Education in 1984, the district knew the population of Hispanics and English language learners was growing. This was no longer a district with a minority but a district where the minority would soon outpace the numbers of white non-ethnic students.

To ensure change was backed by funding, the district had applied for a federally funded Title VII grant. These grants did not pay for teachers, that was the responsibility of the local district, but they did provide for materials, professional development and supplementary staffing such as counselors and remedial specialists.

The Title VII grant application resulted in a new design for Bilingual Education in Windham. The concept of The Connecticut Pairing Model came into the school districts hosting a majority of the English- language learners in the state. With this model, the pairs stayed in place, but all instruction originated with the Spanish- classroom teachers at each grade level. In short, the English teacher keyed off the Spanish teacher, who initiated learning units. The lack of materials was well known and, as most of the teachers had ties to the Island, they sent back for the books and curriculum guides approved for use in Puerto Rico. Those little books were Xeroxed and used to teach reading in the elementary school. Children read about Puerto Rico; it's climate, animals, vegetables and minerals, its history, and its famous people. Their parents had learned from the same books, and they were enchanted with the idea of really being part of their children's education. The idea did not follow as well into secondary school as on the Island; students do not study United States history until they reach their junior year in high school.

In 1984, the same problems of time in program and learning gaps were evident. At a Board of Education meeting, one Board member said to me in total exasperation, "Can't you just say CAT and then spell it?" A principal spoke very slowly and very, very loudly to make a connection. Others offered simultaneous translation as a strategy. Yet another administrator suggested repeating everything over and over until it was mastered. There was no paucity of layman's advice. Understanding of the process of learning a second language was almost as limited with teachers. As a recent graduate of a Master's Program in Second Language Learning I was possibly the only administrator who had read something in the field. No one was to blame for this; Universities were slow in realizing the need for such an addition to traditional syllabi.

It was time for some changes in both the bilingual program classes and in the mainstream. The number of years "in program" was an issue at the State Department of Education level. All districts had to send annual reports breaking down the numbers of identified English language learners in bilingual programs by year, date of entry and special needs. The data analysis provoked a huge outcry; children were in the program too many years. Brushed aside was the fact that they were learning content-based English as well as content in Spanish. And it is also true that many students needed to move on. The rub was the lack of training of mainstream teachers who felt that if a student was assigned to their classroom that child should be on a level with all other students. Acronyms were developed to sort out this situation so in addition to LEP (Limited English Proficient) NEP (Newly English Proficient) and FEP (Fully English Proficient) were added to the lexicon. Rubrics were developed to sort out proficiency levels but only the bilingual teachers administered the tests leaving mainstream teachers with little information when students were scheduled for classes.

Special Education for non-English speakers was an unresolved problem – should they be taught solely in English or in a language they understood? At the time, English was the preferred route and the lack of certified bilingual Special Education teachers made this necessary. At one close-out IEP session, the special education teacher reported that a student had learned the five sounds of "a" during the school year. This was his sole accomplishment.

If the problem was length of time in the bilingual program, what was the solution that avoided failure in the mainstream? Another acronym, PMS, came into being. Later, a teacher told me of the double meaning of PMS but for a year or two it meant partial mainstreaming. Students were put in mainstream classes where they had strength and some hope of passing: the remainder of their time was in the bilingual program.

At each grade level there were specific issues. At the elementary school the early grades went well. It began to fall apart in 4th grade when the ability to understand and learn from independent reading is essential. And, of course, 4th grade was a typical exit year. At the middle school and high school the English language learners were late arrivals with a variety of academic backgrounds, needs and motivation. There could be no blanket changes, each school was different.

A basic and necessary change to be made was related to the grade assignments. When students mainstreamed, they returned to their districted school. When students reached a higher grade, they returned to their districted school. Unlike their peers, ELLs would probably attend two elementary schools before entering the one Windham Middle School. Another transition for those struggling with the big change from "home" to Connecticut.

EARLY CHILDHOOD: THE FIRST CULTURAL EXCHANGE

The youngest English language learners in the '70's and '80's were in pre-school programs funded under Head Start and local social service agencies. Folk wisdom still persists - it is easier for young children to learn a second language and immersion is good. Explaining the urgency of learning English to a 3- or 4- year old is a frustrating business. They have yet to understand the need for English to get a good job or a college education. These were times when certified early- childhood teachers were not plentiful, and Spanish- speaking- certified early- childhood teachers were even scarcer. By necessity, paraprofessionals who spoke Spanish were hired to support the teachers and to bring some kind of sense to the daily routine.

As an observer it was easy to see that the division of labor in place gave the teacher full control of curriculum and scheduling with the paraprofessionals acting as instructional facilitators. The pre-school program did not follow the bilingual program model. Teachers were

English- speaking and somewhat overwhelmed by the demands of the job. Scenes at the bus line were interesting for the diversity of behavior as well as background. Small as they were, the English speakers stayed in line with minimal back- sliding. Our Spanish speakers walked around, laughed, and enjoyed themselves.

The more the children enjoyed themselves, the more the teachers and bus monitors cried for order, in English. The Spanish speakers did what any sensible person would do: they ignored the background noise as irrelevant.

One wonders where reputations are made. This early start, intended to socialize and provide common basics for the children, resulted in mainstream teachers judging the children unready to learn and children realizing that teachers didn't know everything and should be ignored when speaking loudly. And perhaps this first venture into school gave parents an idea that their children were not going to be shining stars in the public schools. In the end, the parents disillusionment lasted longest; they resigned themselves to years of problems with school.

In 2007, the Frank Porter Graham Child Development Institute at the University of North Carolina at Chapel Hill released findings corroborating the idea that English-only policies may not promote success for Spanish speaking pre-schoolers. The article begins, "Contrary to conventional wisdom, English only pre-kindergarten classrooms may not help native Spanish-speaking children become better prepared for school. Observers for the Institute noted that Spanish-speaking students experienced less aggression, bullying and teasing by their classmates when Spanish was included in their educational development. The author of this study, Gisele Crawford, stated that many early childhood programs leave English language learners at risk of social and language problems.

Still, conventional wisdom seems to win out in many states where the introduction to school includes a full rejection of the first years of a child's development if it happened in a language other than English.

The focus on early childhood is happening once again. Researchers are bringing the question of English into the picture but it may not be left unframed. Salaries for pre-school teachers should be raised, along with the training and accreditation of those who choose to work with our youngest language learners. It is time to examine the things we know, for example, that when reading begins in an unknown language the experience itself makes no sense. The children lose their sense of themselves as "learners" if only English at its most basic level is considered important. Literacy has been the goal of public education for many years to ensure lifetime learning for the citizens of our country. It is never too early to start equating reading with being part of the development of each individual.

Elementary School

Staffing was a problem but the network came into play, and eventually teams were available for one elementary school now ready to implement the Pairing Model. The idea of Spanish-speaking teachers as the lead instructors was as novel then as it is now. Many of the teachers were new to New England, indeed they were new to the mainland, and many were English- language learners themselves. Thirty years later, a few are still in place, and they are master teachers, community leaders, and advocates for children.

Teacher training reinforced the need for Spanish first before moving the curriculum into English. The idea was to create seamless units of study, transitioning students from learning in Spanish to continuing to learn the same material in English. Materials in Spanish were almost non-existent, but the enthusiasm of teachers for translation and the arrival of well-known readers from Puerto Rico brought the new program into being. Certainly there were no content texts in Spanish and few storybooks. The Lectura was heavy on phonics and facts about the Island.

These reading books had been those used by the teachers on the Island and their own reading had started with the Lectura. It was familiar to parents, teachers, and all staff involved with the Spanish part of the program.

The scant quantity of research was apparent at the university level. Many theories were in place, but they held no force. Years of research could not be cited, nor could findings on the worth of native language instruction, it wasn't there. What was also apparent was the failure rate of Hispanic students, in the early grades and into high school. Early on, there were several groups whose constituents were scandalized by teaching children in Spanish in an "American" school. Most teachers were willing to try anything that might help the children learn.

The initiation of the Connecticut Mastery Tests in grades 4, 6, and 8 changed the landscape. While the students were learning English, their scores on the Connecticut Mastery Tests (CMTs) were well below those of their peers. It was understood that the test items were not favorable to children who were unfamiliar with beavers and pilgrims, and an attempt to sensitize the tests was handed to a committee. It did help somewhat, however, determining the culture of a word or a section of reading is a major challenge.

Language was still a large part of the problem. On one 4th grader's test, the directions had asked for students to draw four angles. The resulting drawing was of four simple but recognizable angels, topped with halos.

It is difficult to assess all the things that can go wrong with administering a standardized test to a non-native English speaker. The idea of translating the test into

Spanish did not go far. The idea of giving non-English speakers a standardized Spanish test at grade level did not excite State Department of Education officials either. And so year after year, those children classified bilingual or LEP continued to do far worse than their classmates. Several nationally renowned researchers eventually made their voices heard, noting that the same children were not classified in the Limited English category each year. Newcomers assured districts of sizable numbers, but students exited and entered the testing base. Dr. Linquati is speaking now to the need to follow the progress of individuals, not established categories.

Dr. Virginia Collier called the question in several ways. In a speech many years past, she pointed out that the 50th percentile means, by definition, that 50% of the children tested will be below and 50% will be above the median. You can be sure of the groups that are below. Her second very serious observation was that "closing the gap" was not quite the easy goal imagined. While LEP (a Federal term) students are learning, their peers are not sitting still waiting for them. Each group learns and moves up the ladder but the gap remains.

The advent of accountability in state reporting brought the benefits of the Connecticut Pairing Model under review. The attempts to educate children in the language they understood were admirable and right, but the longer goal was to educate children to succeed in their new home. They needed more than the social English of the playground; they needed to be able to function and learn in academic English. The break through of Dr. Jim Cummins, who separated language learning into Basic Interpersonal Communication (BICs) and Cognitive

Academic Proficiency (CALP) skills, was significant to every district and to Windham as well.

The Connecticut Pairing Model was modified to ensure that children learning English as a second language were instructed in the same curricula as their classmates in the "mainstream" program. This was a standard term used by writers in the field, federal government grants, and districts across the country. We wanted the English learners to have the opportunity to succeed in the mainstream; the current programs were not geared to that path.

The State Department of Education moved to limit enrollment in a program of bilingual education to 30 months. This made it essential that they enter mainstream classrooms with most of the prior knowledge their peers had learned over time.

Luckily, materials had been advancing over time as bilingual education became a nation-wide response to legal action demanding equal educational opportunities for non-English- speaking children. There was a chance. It was possible to find text books published in two languages so that content was the same in math and science. Trade books came out in both Spanish and English. Students could read Sarah Plain and Tall in the mainstream in English and in bilingual programs in Spanish. The number of publishers increased each year, ending the reliance on out-dated or culturally biased materials from Argentina and Spain. Federal Grants under Title VII funded well-designed programs that acted as models for districts struggling to adapt. With money to spend, educators of English language learners could buy materials without relying on hard- strapped local districts to duplicate books in Spanish and English.

Kindergarten- and First- grade teachers in Windham found that they could beat the state's 30- month timeline and produce early readers who deciphered both English and Spanish. Two teachers of exceptional expertise were Rosa Tirado and Noemi Alers. Their children made excellent progress and most moved into mainstream classrooms. How long it took for them to forget the Spanish part of their resume is unknown but few of these students remained literate in Spanish after third grade. The rub, of course there is one, is that when the use of the two languages ended, the children learned only in English and they still lacked some of the prior cultural knowledge leaned on by peers and teachers in the mainstream classrooms.

In 1983, Kathy Friedman wrote a paper on counseling needs in Grades K-8. Kathy, a bilingual teacher, was able to interview a great number of people in the language they preferred. Her paper was divided into groups and the first group reported was composed of the students themselves.

Students responded to a question on entering the regular classroom with a fear that they would not be able to understand enough English to do the work. They also feared that Americans (sic) would "pick on them". Nearly every student interviewed stated in different ways that they weren't as capable of doing the work as their Anglo peers. One girl responded, "You need help if you're in the bilingual program. You're smarter when you go into the regular program". Students who had exited into the mainstream program noted that they participated in more activities when they went to regular classes.

Parents wanted their children to maintain the Puerto Rican culture and language; they wanted Americans to accept their children; they hoped the children would learn English well. Many parents felt estrangement from their children after they learned to speak English well. Some felt their children had assumed the role of parents.

Teacher perceptions were markedly different between mainstream and bilingual faculty. All recognized the significance of English but program teachers saw either subtle or overt discrimination. In order for transition to be successful, Puerto Rican teachers noted a host of psychological, emotional and academic needs to be addressed. Anglo teachers wanted exit as soon as English was tested competent for mainstreaming. Although both groups felt low socio-economic status was an issue, bilingual program teachers cited the low-self esteem Windham Latinos held due to the inferior social status of Puerto Ricans on the mainland. One teacher particularly noted that what sets Puerto Ricans apart from the previous waves of immigrants is that they come to the mainland with the expectation that equal opportunities be accorded them as enfranchised American citizens.

Problems were freely discussed. Bilingual program teachers who followed their former students found that misbehavior by Hispanics in the mainstream was a coping strategy for feelings of rejection. Creating disturbances and disobedience legitimized the anxieties about being outcasts for both boys and girls. An observant Anglo teacher characterized this type of situation by saying,

"Just because there's integration, there's not necessarily interaction."

Puerto Rican boys often were considered head of the household. As their English allowed them to be the main spokesperson linking the family to the various agencies in the community, this was certainly true in part. The boy might also have friends who pushed him into proving his manhood through fighting. If it is a choice of fitting into the Anglo world or the culture of the Puerto Rican community there was not a big decision to make.

School Counselors and Psychologists interviewed were all Anglo. Their feeling echoed concerns of bilingual program teachers. Students should not be fully exited and new timelines, including gradual mainstreaming, should be initiated. Group sessions for students and parents could help the process succeed and perhaps assist family members remain a cohesive unit. In Puerto Rico, mothers depend on extended family to raise children. On the mainland, mothers often headed single parent homes and the Pentecostal church in Willimantic might be their only network for the reinforcement of social and cultural values. Human Service Agencies and social workers saw the breakdown of the extended family, parent-child value conflict, lack of school and discrimination as the primary causes of the bilingual student's failure to succeed.

Administrators were as one in recognizing the need for bilingual services. A principal indicated that bilingual program students formed excessively dependent ties to the Puerto Rican teachers and to Latino peers. One proposed solution was to integrate specials such as art, music and physical education. Other remedies included accurate assessments of progress; clear reclassification procedures, provision of transitional services and gradual mainstreaming. An emphasis on family/school communication was repeatedly cited as a problem impeding bilingual program student success in the mainstream.

Ms. Friedman, in her analysis, noted that without a system-wide commitment to multicultural appreciation no initiatives would be successful agents of change.

THE MIDDLE SCHOOL

In the 1991-92 school year, Kramer Middle School served grades 6-8 with a total enrollment of 745 boys and girls. Fifty-four students were placed in a program of bilingual education; thirty-three students received ESL support. There were two Hispanic (State term) teachers on the professional staff.

The big buzz in bilingual education in the late '70's was relevance. Teachers should draw on the children's background knowledge to involve them in the educational process.

A bilingual program student, new but learning fast, asked why she had to keep hearing about the Tainos. She would be interested to hear about U.S. history where she knew nothing. The Tainos were old friends. Relevance means knowing what your peers know even if it is not part of your background.

Students in these vulnerable years reacted in different ways. They were looking at the best ways to survive in adolescence, not an easy task for any pre-teen. The boys became macho, the girls moved toward the idea of beginning their own family.

When I left the Middle School classroom, students were scheduled by English proficiency. It made sense but a new ESL teacher, Ann Anderberg, worked with the Principal to improve learning by teaching English in content. This meant grouping students by grade level to bring the appropriate curriculum into play. An ESL classroom held a wide range of English abilities but a Puerto Rican characteristic is to help your friends. This was a philosophical shift designed to prepare more students for mainstreaming; it took the emphasis off of learning English as a language to learning the content of Connecticut curriculum. The real transition to content over language was happening in these years. Publishers were quick to capitalize on the change and books titled Learning English in the Content areas were popular.

The goal of mainstreaming with a similar academic background as peers was on target, especially as materials were available. The number of publishers providing content, fiction and non-fiction in Spanish and English increased every year. Middle School was on the fringe, most of the publishers concentrated on elementary school, but science and math books in both languages were available for the middle grades.

Partial mainstreaming was in place with a transition teacher available to support students who were starting out. A mainstream teacher was asked what he would like to see in a mainstreamed student. His response was that the exited child should have the same level of reading and writing skills in English as all the other students. The idea that being placed in the mainstream was considered an accelerant to begin to close the gap was not in most mainstream teacher's understanding.

Teachers who could successfully integrate the students ready to make the move into regular classrooms were there and they became the core of transition. The school had a strong principal and an experienced ESL teacher. A transition teacher was there for support. It seemed to be on the right track but scores on the Connecticut Mastery Test were significantly lower than the mainstream and had a distressing tendency to rise spectacularly one year making the next year's drop heart breaking. Accommodations offered to ELLs included more time, sometimes the use of dictionaries. As a test observer, I watched the bent heads and scratching pencils thinking that this time all would be well. I asked one student his strategy after the tests were collected. "Well" he said seriously, "I do an A, then B, then C. Then I do C, B, and A. You know, mix them up." Multiple choice testing has flaws.

Eighth grade graduation was a true rite of passage, following the tradition of the Island. Student came in semi-formal suits and gowns, mixing with the other students who wore school day clothes with a little more starch. Awards were given and at last, Hispanic and Bilingual Program students began to collect their rewards. These graduations were special.

At the close of the first year of high school, few of these graduates had enough credits to be classified as sophomores. By the end of 10th grade, many had reached the 16th year landmark for leaving school. And they did. I had an argument with a principal about 9th grade being the highest dropout year. We were both right.

In January of 1997 the entire Kramer Middle School staff, administration and students walked to a new technologically advanced Windham Middle School on Quarry Street. The new building and its playing fields looked down on Sweeney Elementary. It was prime real estate and architecturally perfect for the new century. A Task Force had been formed to complete a self-study called the Middle Grade School State Policy Initiative, sponsored by the Carnegie Foundation. Clay Krevolin was Principal and his Steering Committee included the most dedicated and knowledgeable of the Middle School staff.

The High School

For all students, the ability to pass content classes in English was less a problem than English class itself. On the Island, American History is not in the curriculum until junior year of high school. Imagine the background information every child in a US school has accumulated over 10 years, beginning with the Pilgrims first Thanksgiving and carrying on through World Wars and student protests. These two may seem unrelated but literature presupposes cultural knowledge new arrivals did not have.

English presented a problem as their accumulated credits resulted in freshman status despite years in residence. Four years of English were required to graduate. The schedule of classes held all the elements for failure. Teachers were mired in "standards" and having the same curriculum, grading premises, and expectations for all. Good to a point. High expectations have never been the root of student failure. Providing a way for them to achieve high academic standards is the issue.

It became clear that the very best students, those who came late from the Island with excellent grades and strong records in content areas, were having the hardest emotional time in mainstream classes although their content knowledge was good. In part, this was happening because of their own high standards. They were not used to being at the bottom of the ranks. Another part of the problem was the reaction of peers, and sometimes, teachers, to mistakes in speaking and writing.

The appropriate solution was to accept ESL as an English credit. This required a substantial ESL curriculum covering the same elements as the mainstream English classes. As this had been slowly developed using current research on teaching English through content it was possible. By the '80s materials were available to match the literature of mainstream English with abridged versions, videos and when possible, the original books translated into Spanish.

NEASC and The Race/ Culture Retreats

The ten year review for accreditation was upon Windham High School. Teachers used this exercise to bring up smoldering concerns unaddressed in the routine running of the school. The Principal, Don Berkowitz, was a dynamo, administrating and also teaching when he felt unconnected to the faculty and unimpressed with the progress students were making in algebra. The visitors from the New England Association of Secondary Schools was just another way to connect and he was more than ready.

Windham did well. The most pressing issue was school climate. The fuzzy issues of cultural disconnect still hovered through the halls, cafeteria, and classrooms. Some teachers felt integration was slow in coming, others saw the process of mainstreaming as essentially unfair. And students had their own perceptions of faculty judgment.

A solution was developed with the assistance of Bert Phillips, a trained professional who helped districts address such problems. He was black, he was from Bermuda and he fit the school. His prompting resulted in a series of Race/Culture Seminars first attended by faculty and later by students. As few of the teachers were minority at that time, it seemed a bit one-sided to me: the focus seemed to be on changing the students to conform to what was there. Some students disliked being discussed impersonally but they waited to see if change was a possibility.

There was more awareness of differences and some new and surprising experiences. When the students turn for a Seminar came, the program moved to the University of Connecticut campus so that dormitories could house everyone. UConn students were not the most welcoming hosts and the Windham crew could not ignore the comments aimed at them. What was to be a refreshing focus on cultural differences through shared discussion was shaped by the outside world and it did open the eyes of some teachers who participated. The students were less surprised and less likely to join in the exercise after returning home.

On Thursday, April 14th, 1988 a Symposium on Racism in Our Multicultural Society was held at Windham High School. It was sponsored by the Windham Education Association and organized by Mary Phelps, the English teacher who suffered through the early pilot of American Folklore for English language learners. David Carter, President of Eastern Connecticut State University was the lead speaker. President Carter, one of first black university presidents in Connecticut, was educated at Central State University in Wilberforce, Ohio. His M.A. in education was awarded at Miami University in Oxford , Ohio and his PhD from Ohio State University. Before assuming the

Presidency of ECSU, Dr. Carter was Associate Dean of the School of Education at the University of Connecticut and then Vice-President for Academic Affairs. His knowledge of the process of education, the administrative process and the unique problems of minorities gave the evening a significant introduction to the problems faced in Windham. Bert Phillips, our original Race-Culture consultant came back to join the symposium.

Participants included the Program Associate for Affirmative Action at UConn, a counselor in the Department of Counseling Services at UConn, a bilingual psychologist working with United Social and Mental Health Services in Willimantic, the Rabbi at Temple Bnai Israel in Willimantic and the Director of the Windham Public Schools Bilingual Program.

All of these people had seen the results of racism in their lives and careers. The audience was full; it was a night of distinguished speakers and participants. And all of us who spoke gave testimony to the damage racism can do to everyone, and especially to young people. There was not one person in the auditorium who didn't believe changes could be made.

David Fenn, A WHS student sang You've Got To Be Carefully Taught from South Pacific, Ricardo Moraga, a bilingual program teacher sang Guantanamera and the Calvary Baptist Church Choir sang Move Mountainss.

These are all people of good will but it was eleven years since the Race Culture Seminars and still there was work to be done.

Intercambia: A
Cultural Exchange

In the mid 80's, the Connecticut State Department of Education and the Department of Education in Puerto Rico set up an exchange program. In 1988, teachers across Connecticut were recruited to spend three weeks in August on the Island, learning about the educational system and society that produced many of their current students.

Five educators from Windham were eager to go. Ann, Nereida, Ed, Bill, and I left hot and sticky Connecticut in the company of 30 teachers, administrators, and State Department of Education officials, arriving at Isla Verde on a windy and mellow summer day. We were bussed to Aquadilla, site of a former army facility, complete with barracks and a cafeteria.

Exotic lizards decorated the walls of the barracks, welcoming us each morning with close eye contact. We shared their home without conflict. Stray dogs congregated outside the compound. Ann and I smuggled bits of food out each day, making friends we were sorry to leave behind.

Daily lectures from each Cabinet Office in the Puerto Rican government began at 9:00 a.m. The officials drove in from Hato Rey each morning, on time, dressed in suits and ties, ready to explain the workings of the Island. They were well prepared, overwhelming us with facts and figures.

The Connecticut group was together this first week. Everyone took something different from the lectures but they were impressive. The problems of "Neo-Ricans" were serious. While stateside schools grappled with non-English speakers, the Island saw equal numbers of non-Spanish speakers returning "home" without language or academic skills. Remedial Spanish, Spanish as a second language, tutoring, special school programs, and even special schools were developed to address the academic and language problems of new arrivals.

And so these children of the "Air Bus" posed a problem on both sides of the water. If you assume that mobility is part of the Puerto Rican experience, one trip and one solution would not be of great help these students were citizens, free to move back and forth. Unlike immigrants who took the trip as a one-way ticket, losing Spanish meant limiting opportunity and contact with their extended families. Most of the Island students went past secondary school through the community college or college system. Those returning from schools in the USA were lost in the competition, prepared only for lower level jobs or no jobs at all.

The concerns of educators on the Island extended past content and language to values. A curriculum for values was under construction mostly for the returnees who were on a different wave length than their Island reared peers. Those returning were of all grades and ages, just as they are still in mainland schools. This was a major initiative for Island educators who found that character building was a necessity. On this side of the water, Building Character in Crisis is the title of an article written by Patrick F. Bassett, Paul D. Houston, and Rushworth M. Kidder in 2009. They find fraud, bribery and moral integrity a problem for mainland ethics. They cite Governor Rod Blagojevich of Illinois, arrested for soliciting bribes to fill a U.S. Senate seat vacated by President Barack Obama, and Bernard L. Madoff who ran a $65 billion Ponzi scheme. The issue of character goes deep into who we are as a country, what we value and how we care for one another. On the Island, the numbers of Neo-Ricans brought this issue to a head over twenty years ago but it was more a question of classroom discipline than loss of a moral compass.

As the officials of Puerto Rico's State Department of Education spoke, their knowledge of their own crisis became clear. The Director of Title I described the use of funding to teach English. In many classrooms students had a mastery of English that surpassed that of their teachers. They were the unruly element for children on the Island are expected to respect their teachers and their parents reinforce this respect. On the mainland, Title I is used to help students who need support in academics. We heard about the historic moment in Puerto Rican history when English was the mandated language of instruction. Classes were taught in English by teachers who were learning the language as they taught. Small wonder that Puerto Ricans did poorly on English based IQ tests, providing a convenient excuse for low expectations and profiling.

Curriculum for all grades and all schools was distributed from the Central Offices in Hato Rey. In one sense it was restrictive and there were few books to supplement the written guides. In another, it brought continuity to the children who frequently moved around on the Island itself. All students in grade 4 were learning the same content in each academic area no matter where they lived. On the mainland, a simple move within a district could bring a new reading series and even a new method of sequencing math instruction.

The teaching profession itself was highly sought but salaries were unbelievably low. A little over $1,000 per month was considered a median. No ties of tenure bound districts, which were all governed by Central Office and subject to the political parties in power. Continuity of teaching staff was a myth.

Into the Classrooms

After the week of lectures in the morning and evening with afternoons free for exploring, the group was split and moved to host homes around the Island. My hostess was from Rincon and so the schools she chose to visit were in the western corner of Puerto Rico. The hosts were responsible for two weeks of guests, stressing out families who lived in small homes. My hostess had been pressed into service despite a dying grandmother and anxious parents. Blanca was an English as a Second Language teacher and together we left the house before the family rose, returning each night about 10:00 p.m. after the family retired. It was a hard schedule but everyone helped make it work.

We visited schools in towns near the ocean and high in the mountains. We saw technical schools and a special school built to serve those in care because of family or legal problems. In every school the lack of books and supplies was evident.

A vocational education teacher showed us his room. He had one textbook and his personal toolbox. He told us that his challenge was to plan projects that didn't require materials and he said it with a smile. I thought of union organizers but didn't smile.

At every school we visited, students presented us with gift: a ceramic coqui, a bonita bandera, an autograph book signed withtheir names. I have them all. In one mountain school the principal met us at the end of the road. I couldn't see any school but the principal was dressed to perfection with high heels and a bright smile. As I floundered up and down muddy hills to the many buildings composing this school, she remained cool, calm, graceful, and patient. At this school, our Connecticut group was partially reunited,our schedules overlapping.

The English teacher we visited had lived on the mainland and was equal to facing 40 tightly packed English-language learners in each class. In other classes, students knew more than the teachers, they were the neo-Ricans who had English as their dominant language, sometimes their only language. As the Central Office people had noted, the number of Spanish language learners returning from the mainland was formidable.

After several hours of classroom visits, presentations, and speeches, we met in the cafeteria with the hosts and the principal. We were talking and suddenly Bill began to sing Danny Boy in his clear Irish tenor. Instant silence in the huge cafeteria until the last note faded.The song lingered as we said good-bye; it was a special exchange that needed no words at all.

The next stop was Moca. This small city had a total population of 7,033 students in 22 schools: 4,060 in elementary school, 1,714 in Intermediate and 1,168 in high school. Special Education students broke down at 42 in elementary, 93 in Intermediate and 101 in the high school. As a percentage it is easy to see that although some student stayed the course, the numbers requiring support grew at each level. Intermediate school ended at grade 9 and it was a significant, certified graduation. Not all the students would move on. The enthusiasm for 8th grade graduation in Windham was clarified - this was a checkpoint for students at home, we never realized its importance.

At the intermediate school we observed a class and then had a summary of the lesson from Sr. Antonio Pedreira, the teacher. This was a 7th grade classroom in Chapter I English for beginning students. Lesson structure included a review and an exercise in stretching sentences. The objective of the lesson was the use of contractions - not a feature of the Spanish language. The teacher spent some time on direct instruction, and then modeling with whole group participation, guided practice in small groups and then independent practice with the oversight of a constantly moving teacher. It was a seamless lesson and all of the students were on task throughout the hour we were with them.

The next school was an Escuela Superior - a white washed high school with a central courtyard and many flowers in and around. The sounds of insects, animals and birds competed with the sounds coming from the classrooms. In effect, outside was inside. Students came late to class but quietly and without interrupting the teacher or their classmates. Their day was shorter, at that time many schools operated on a split schedule to accommodate everyone. This school in Moca had an ambiance that was palpable. Students were happy. Sr. Wilfredo Soto was the Director of the Escuela Superior Moca and he did his job well.

Although classrooms were structured and attention demanded, there were frequent breaks, an hour and a half for lunch and the availability of a store and possibly a piragua cart close by the school grounds. The central courtyard was open and free to parents who sometimes brought lunch to their children. There was nothing called Physical Education - sports were for after school hours. Baseball leagues abounded and our own Windham team made a visit to Puerto Rico to play teams in the leagues.

The teachers we saw were dedicated and energetic. Absences were few: if a teacher was absent, no class was held. They had few materials but they had curriculum guides from Central Office and the full support of parents. The greatest memory of visits to the schools was of the courtesy and hospitality of the administrators and teachers, matched only by the courtesy and warmth of the students. And it should be recorded here that, despite the limitations, a high percent of high school graduates went on to higher education and today, the number is significantly higher than the mainland USA.

Hasta la Vista

On the last day, Blanca took me to the beach at Rincon. Across the street from the beach sat a Spanish- style white stucco building with a red tile roof. This was Rincon's high school, surrounded by palms and hibiscus facing the sea with serenity. The water was blue green, buoyant and warm. Blanca brought a chair, a scarf, and a large hat. She sat under the palms watching for sharks while I had my last swim. I swam, looking back at the school and thinking of the newcomers of last January, climbing over the snowdrifts of Willimantic. Finally it was time to go back to the barracks and board the buses to the airport and home.

Those educators who came to learn did. Others found ways to reinforce prejudices. The next summer participants would host their hosts. We were in agreement that we could never match the hospitality we had experienced.

RETURN TO CONNECTICUT

We had been gone for three weeks. While we enjoyed the cool breezes on the beach of Aguadilla and the crisp mornings in the mountains, Connecticut had been experiencing a predictable heat wave. School was imminent. There were workshops to plan, assignments to double check, classrooms to observe for blackboards, materials and organization. A return to reality that should be helped by what we had learned. Neri still mourned our failure to see the Caves at Camuy, Ann would probably have stayed on, Bill and Ed looked relieved as we waved good-by.

It seemed we had left on summer vacation and returned to the full push of school opening. As usual, there were staff decisions to address, grant reports to write, professional development to plan, State mandated testing of new possible limited English students to schedule and requests for materials to fill. Assessment was always a large time commitment.

The rules required new students to complete a Home Language Survey, and at this point these surveys were on file for every, I mean every, student in the district except newcomers. In the elementary school classroom teachers were responsible, at the Middle School, homeroom teachers took on the task, and in the High School, English teachers were notified of those needing to complete a simple form asking what the first language of the student was and what was the language spoken at home. This triggered mandatory testing on the Language Assessment Survey (LAS) that determined whether a student might qualify for Bilingual Education. If so, parents had the option of choosing the special bilingual program or the mainstream classrooms.

Many districts moved children in a form of bilingual redistricting to avoid the need for a bilingual program. In fact, Windham began a push towards redistricting in order to better spread the LEP children around all four elementary schools. The rationale was to allow integration and to give the district schools equal numbers of minority students.One excellent outcome was providing enough students in each building to end the practice of moving our mainstreaming LEP students from one school to another when they were ready to exit the bilingual program. All schools enroll part of the program then and they do today.

The Business of the Day

Central Office required a larger perspective. Instead of my own familiar group at the high school there were thirty-five teachers and many children to plan for. It had a life outside of the school as well.

Early in the fall of 1985, one Council member asked if we were considering a policy statement on AIDs as an entry in the Big Book of policies. A new Superintendent intern took it as a chance to joke that such modern ailments would not come to Willimantic, they were part of the big city scenes. And so no policy was made.It took less than a year for Windham Hospital to treat its first case of AIDS. HIV had found the quiet corner. Now some kind of policy became imperative. The larger cities in Connecticut had addressed this so there were models to follow. Advice from laymen and professional health personnel was freely given. Could we exclude children with HIV, children with parents with HIV? No, was the unequivocal answer.

The first measure involved ordering cartons of rubber gloves that were distributed to schools and then to classrooms. Any body fluids, and there are plenty at all schools, were to trigger an instant reaction: rubber gloves. Those teachers with latex intolerance could only hope their students maintained a complete skin covering, intestinal fortitude and a lack of seasonal colds. The relief of passing out the plastic protectors soon passed as it was found that there were babies being born who were HIV positive and parents who were dealing with full cases of AIDs.

I think the shock of dealing with the disease wore off and normal behaviors returned. I am sure teachers still have pairs of plastic coverings in their desk drawers but I doubt they are used. We learn to live with anything, it takes only time.

"What Do You Do All Day? " a teacher asked. The usual chores and responsibilities of administration were scheduled. With almost 35 staff members in the six Windham schools, mandated evaluation sessions three times a year took a good amount of time. These were special chances to see the children as well. Evaluation guidelines were determined by administrators and teachers on three levels: non-tenured lesson implementation and performance objectives, tenured implementation, or professional development projects described by teacher and administrator in September. The greatest value was touching base individually with the teachers who were guiding student progress. Our teachers were bilingual with few exceptions. Some teachers had English as a first language; others were native Spanish speakers. The teachers came from many Spanish-speaking locales: Puerto Rico, Haiti, Mexico, Spain, Colombia, Peru and others I can't recall. Contrary to popular myth, all of them understood each other. With the exception of accent, idiom and cultural references, Spanish was a language of communication shared with the professionals, the children and the parents.

Meetings consumed another chunk of time. Central Office meetings, budget meetings, principal meetings to address school problems with the bilingual program, Special Education meetings, meetings with Specials teachers, meetings with parents, meetings with community groups. Required as well was a mandated Board of Education meeting each month. And leaving the local scene brought more meetings with the State Department of Education (SDE), State Directors, National conferences and required workshops for grant holders.

State mandated testing for bilingual program children took time, training for testers, ordering appropriate tests, sending out the tests and receiving the results to be incorporated in reports. Results needed to be analyzed to change student placements and instruction. The tests for pre-school through high school Spanish speaking students were required by the State and by the Federal funding that came through grants. In addition to the testing in Spanish, bilingual program students also were tested in English, and when the Connecticut Mastery Tests came through, they were tested on grade level the same as their English speaking peers. Those tests were also analyzed and reported on with no great enthusiasm.

Reports had to be written for the SDE annually and early on, grants needed to be re-applied for each year, regardless the length of time the award stipulated. New grants needed to be written to keep the program intact. An electric typewriter was state of the art. Imagine the finality of typing down goals, objectives and activities when a single change could mean retyping many pages. There was white-out but sometimes a quick correction was not enough. I stopped bringing applications to the Superintendent for approval until the deadline was so close there was no question of changes. Windham's Superintendent in those years had been an English major, who could locate errors on every page. I have no quarrel with him, he was usually right. Actually, that was more acceptable than finding one error that could bring the whole project back to the typewriter. When I was given a computer discarded by Curriculum, life was good. Unfortunately, in the middle of a grant application the computer gave up. The load it had carried under Curriculum was simply too much. It was tired. That grant application had to be started all over as no one could save what had been done to another disc – the computer was completely frozen.

It was surely more fun to be teaching and I missed my high school students. On the other had, working with adults could be productive too and getting to know the teachers of the program well was a bonus.

During those years I worked with four elementary schools, one middle school and one high school, the Headstart program and St. Mary's in Willimantic. St. Mary's was added to the list as a Chapter I school that needed to be monitored by the public school district. When Chapter I observers came to the building, all pictures of a religious nature had to be removed from the walls in the Chapter I classroom. Sister Domenica would sadly say, "I will do this but it isn't right".

Of all the responsibilities and duties of the job the only one I would complain about daily was the parking situation. The search for a parking slot was fine in good weather, a total disaster in the snow.

PART III.

THE DUAL LANGUAGE PROGRAM

Quien habla dos lenguas, vale por dos.

Dual Language

The answer for some of the problems for our English language learners could be found in Dual Language Programs. Why have a subtraction of knowledge in school? Why should any American child not enjoy the benefits of literacy in two languages? Why not a program that integrates children of both languages and teaches in both?

By May of 1992 a report had been prepared and delivered to the Board of Education. A committee was formed to study the ramifications of implementing such a program and the process began. I had visited schools with such programs in Washington, D.C. and Albuquerque New Mexico and also had the excellent research on many Dual Language schools up-dated regularly by the Center for Applied Linguistics in Washington. It was brought to the attention of the Board that European countries had such programs for decades and that consultants from Germany and Sweden were brought to the USA to assist in setting up programs in the United States.

In 1992, thirty school districts in the USA had total or partial immersion programs at the elementary level. Windham was ready. Excellent materials in Spanish were now available. The State Department of Education had developed core curriculum for subjects covered in elementary school that were already used as a base for learning in the program of bilingual education. And, even more important, a number of well-trained Spanish speaking teachers were employed by the Windham Public Schools. Foreign language classes started in grade 7: the dual language program would begin in Kindergarten.

Superintendent Patrick Proctor set up a committee of staff and Board members to look at the cost, space, transportation and enrollment factors involved in the pilot. Windham would have the first Dual Language Program in the state, as the local newspaper called it, "a beacon for Windham's children – and children across the state."

The Board of Education Chair, Judy Hulin, summarized the discussion among Board members as showing excitement and promising support. A result of the meeting was a suggestion that more information should go out to the community for current kindergartners and the parents of four year olds. I announced that the pilot program was slated to begin in January 1993.

PREPARING THE PILOT PROGRAM

A progress report made its way through administrators and Board of Education. The schedule of events is worth listing: it was an extensive period of planning and more important, bringing all participants on board. In May, 1992, the first group went to visit the AMIGOS dual language program at Maynard School in Cambridge, Massachusetts. Follow up sessions with the teachers, administrators and parents who went followed in June and again in August. Informational meetings for parents were set for September, fliers went home in October to the target families and parent conferences with current teachers came throughout November and on request of parents.

Space was available – the contents of the classroom would be changed in existing rooms. Teachers were assigned but they did not respond with any great enthusiasm. This was change in a comfortable program and it might not work as well. Transportation had to be determined. If the program were to be open to all parents' children, could the district provide bussing between schools? And how would the programs we had talked about with the Board be implemented in Windham?

Laidlaw, our school bus vendor, came to the table early as children were able to join the program from any school in the district. As parents signed on, Laidlaw plugged them into the bus routes. A very large group of parents chose to leave Natchaug School in the heart of the city and to move their children to Windham Center, a rural suburb.

Visits continued to AMIGOS for new recruits to the program. Several administrators traveled to the Key School Program in Arlington, Virginia. I remember the day well. We were at the airport north of Hartford at 7:30, in the air at 8:00 and sitting before the Principal of Key School promptly at 9:00 a.m. We also visited the Center for Applied Linguistics to ensure several sources of help during our first years.

Many meetings with parents, alone and in groups, made the month of November pass quickly. In December, the last meetings with the parents of the new Compañeros program met, received their bus schedules, and were charmed by Miriam Reynoso, the first program teacher. We were ready to begin.

One truism learned was that each district, each school is unique. The program models described by The Center For Applied Linguistics (CAL) were working well but they were not always a fit with Windham, Connecticut. When I retired from Windham and went on to work with Dual Language programs in other districts as a consultant, this lesson went with me.

I considered our priority enlisting bilingual teacher support. My own credentials were definitely not enough and there were no existing programs in Connecticut. Through national conferences and interest, I had a list of contacts and the best was also the closest. Mary Cazabon, Director of Bilingual Education in Cambridge, Massachusetts, had a viable and exemplary program in place. She opened the doors for visits by the committee, parents and teachers. When some of the Windham teachers did not choose to go to Cambridge, paying for substitutes in Massachusetts allowed Dual Language teachers from the Amigos program to leave their classes for a day to demonstrate just what was working so well. They brought materials, examples of student work and enthusiasm for what they were accomplishing. Cambridge had developed programs in Spanish, Chinese and other exotic languages based on their own population. If there were native speakers of a language other than English, it was considered good reason to institute two-way learning.

They sold the idea to Windham teachers and the other problems became details.

The details took up a great deal of the spring and summer and involved many presentations to the Board of Ed. The details were many. A large hurdle was getting approval to open the program district-wide and to provide the transportation necessary. This was done with only a few Board members concerned with cost. It was critical to me that the program be bilingual and bicultural with a goal of biliteracy. To achieve these goals, the class should be 50-50 English and Spanish speakers who were also part of the culture their language represented. So for the time, Latino children who spoke only English were not in the mix. We did get the numbers and lost only one girl during the first year as she developed "stress hives" according to her grandmom.

The first school chosen to host the pilot was Windham Center. The Superintendent later asked me why I chose this country school over one in the heart of the city. It was an easy answer – many of the English speaking parents would be willing to send their child to the country for an integrated program but not to the city school where the majority of all students were Latino. A new hire brought the program to full credibility. Miriam Reynoso came to us from Massachusetts where she had worked in a Two-Way program. She was fully equipped to start the Windham pilot and she was a magnificent kindergarten teacher.

A committee of bilingual teachers, ESL teachers and mainstream Kindergarten teachers went to Cambridge again to see the source. It was difficult to convince some that we did not have to follow the Cambridge program in every instance: one mainstream teacher objected whenever the Windham model differed. The program was named Compañeros and it still has that name. It was decided that for the pilot, one bilingual teacher could do the job, alternating languages every three days. A hard sell, but we did start with two half-day sessions of Kindergarten, giving us a good base of children.

In Kindergarten, subject was not critical but it would become a question as the grades progressed. Each year the program would grow a grade until the elementary school years were complete. In Kindergarten there would be full integration of the students and the target was a 50-50 use of the languages. Questions of mobility, late entries, the grades at which newcomers could join the program and opportunities after elementary school were all on the agenda.

Other issues were addressed in the pre-program period. A serious conversation revolved around the integration of program children into the life of the schools. Bilingual program children were often isolated. Some principals cited scheduling problems. This could not happen if the new Dual Language program was going to survive. Special needs students would be welcome if they had a learning disability unaffected by language. Title I students were included. As the program grew, I found the benefit to the Latino children went far beyond language learning. One parent asked me during a Parent Advisory Committee meeting who I was doing the program for – without thinking I told him.

Some problems were to arise later but even before the pilot began plans for Professional Development for program and mainstream teachers were in place. The

Parent Advisory Committee brought up excellent ideas for parent networking across languages, and new methods of reporting student progress.

The preparation and input from all staff and parents made presentations to the Board of Education and interviews with the local newspapers fairly easy. We all knew what we were doing. The support and information from the Center for Applied Linguistics was critical for credibility and it gave the seal of approval to our model. A call for parents to enroll went out in the fall of and in January 1992, after the holidays, the program began in Windham. Dora Whitehouse, a parent of a new program participant, responded in an interview with the Chronicle, "It takes down another barrier between kids, so they can become friends sooner than they might otherwise." Judy Martin said that her daughter, Niomie, expected to be able to help her big brother who was having trouble in his third year of high school Spanish. We had recruited a remarkable core of enthusiastic parents and children, I still remember each one in that first class and the way they approached a change in their education.

Intensive planning for first grade began simultaneously with the opening of the pilot Kindergarten. The program had legs, long and short, and it was going to continue.

A snapshot of Windham at that time showed a total enrollment of 3,333. The total number of Hispanic (a SDE term) students was 1,061. Of that number, 379 took part in bilingual programs. In that year, as reported to the State, 66 students had been exited as English proficient, 96 were mainstreamed in some classes with support, and 87 new arrivals entered into the district. There was a great need for bilingual education in Windham: the old program and the new one as well had a distinct presence in the community.

THE SURVEY

Reinforcement came through the Roper Center at the University of Connecticut. In June 1992, the Willimantic Chronicle published a survey conducted by the graduate students in the Survey Research Program at the University of Connecticut in Storrs. The Chronicle requested that three separate subjects be covered in the survey – attitudes towards the state income tax, attitudes towards bilingual education in Willimantic and Windham, and attitudes towards possible economic development for the Willimantic area.

Three teams of students worked on developing a questionnaire for their area that was eventually integrated into a single document. Students drew the samples to be interviewed, conducted the interviews, tabulated the completed interviews and wrote analyses of the survey results.

In the results, surveys completed by phone and in person have been combined. While the sample is small, it was distributed with the 100 personal interviews over 50 separate blocks in Willimantic and the Windhams. The 100 telephone interviews came from all 50 pages of the Willimantic/Windham telephone directory. An effort was made to include unlisted numbers as well.

Half of the students in the Graduate Survey Research Program at UConn are from the USA mainland, the other half are Latin American. This allowed for the translation of the questionnaire into Spanish. If phone calls were made to a Spanish speaker, a Spanish-speaking student was available for the interview. All of the interviews were conducted between February 14th and February 25, 1992.

This survey project was under the direct supervision of Mr. Burns Roper, who, in addition to teaching at UConn was Chairman of the Board of the Roper Organization that conducts the nationally known Roper Polls.

Survey anaysis gave the Windham Public Schools a rating of Fair to Poor citing a need for better-trained teachers, more technology in the instructional plan and a more extensive bilingual education program. 61% felt new schools were not needed – it was a question of quality over quantity. In general, people's opinion about bilingual education and learning second languages was favorable. In fact, 67% of survey respondents favored a policy that would require all students to learn a second language and as early as possible.56% answered yes to the question on whether they would send their children to schools where some students did not speak English. Respondents felt that bilingual education reduced the rate of school dropouts and absenteeism and improved academic achievement test scores. It was also felt that bilingual education helped with the socialization of non-English speakers although more Windham residents as opposed to those in Willimantic, saw bilingual education as fostering isolation. However, most felt that content courses should be taken in English with support.

81% also spoke to the question of whether the program should be offered to non-English speaking students with a decided yes. The survey analysts decided that there was definite support for bilingual education.

Ten years past, in 1984, when I became Director of Bilingual Education, the Superintendent asked me to speak softly and keep a low profile. The time had definitely come to raise the profile and prepare to bring the positive information of the survey analysis to the Board of Education. The chair of the BOE at that time was Judith Hulin, a true visionary, who believed that a Two-Way program might be right for Windham and that the pilot was working.

ENRICHING ALL THE CHILDREN: DUAL LANGUAGE

An important first step was to name the program. The Cambridge Massachusetts program, Amigos, provided a model in many ways. We were fortunate enough to have the help of Mary Cazabon who opened her doors to visits by teachers, Board of Education members and administrators. We could not replicate the name and so decided to call the Windham version of dual language Compañeros. I recently read in Heading South, Looking North, a book sub-titled A Bilingual Journey by Ariel Dorfman, an explanation of the word. It was serendipitous; we chose exactly the right title.Dorfman writes that Compañeros has no true English equivalent because English synonyms do not contain the Spanish word for bread – pan. It is this word, Dorfman explains, that speaks of two people who break bread together, of the trust implicit in the act. We hoped for this relationship with the students and realized it was a necessity for parents and teachers.

I still believe that trust is the anchor. We all had to believe in the worth of the effort. And we also agreed that the program was not cast in stone, it had the luxury of evolving based on how the evaluation of student achievement showed areas needing improvement in program design. One point was solid: the program would mirror the mainstream curriculum allowing a comparison of achievement with peers untouched by the enrichment of a second language. There was a difference. Students in the Dual Language Program consistently scored higher than peers in the mainstream. Perhaps it is the Hawthorne Effect but most probably it is the expansion of learning.

The pilot kindergarten became known as the Compañeros Pioneers. Many stayed with the program as it moved into Windham Middle School. Not all the children were excited about being pioneers. A serious five-year-old boy refused to say one word in English. One fine winter day I was there to hear him say to Nellie, "I like your pink sneakers." Windham was lucky to have a new bilingual teacher from Massachusetts who had taught in a Dual Language program. Miriam Reynoso was a gift to the children, the district and to me. She started the program and gave it the reputation for excellence that carried us into the critical 1st grade.

The Dual Language program bumped up a grade each year. The most difficult year of all was first grade. Parents who were remarkably relaxed with Kindergarten began comparing notes with neighbors and friends about the status of reading progress. Forget the research. Save the program. We bent with the winds of change and began reading in the child's primary language, bringing in a reading specialist for the English speakers while the Spanish dominant children began their reading lessons in Spanish.

In September of 1994, I received a note from an English speaking Compañeros student who had more than mastered writing in English. The note read as follows:

9/27/94

Dear Mrs. Romano,

I am sending you this order for the sience (sic) center that I am setting up. I would like to know if I can have some money to go to Puppy Love for an aquarium.

I will be waiting for an answer.

Love, Nellie

I kept this letter to cheer me up when parent doubts came down on the first grade.

The two teachers were outstanding. They differed in their approach to teaching reading but the bilingual teacher knew how to reach out to her charges and the English teacher was gifted with the ability to make reading a fun experience. Yusomil Bonet and Lynn Frazier share credit for giving the first graders their start in reading. And, it was noted by spring, that many of the children were reading what they understood in the second language as well as their first. When I was called on to explain this phenomenon at a BOE meeting, one member looked unhappy. Asked what she didn't understand she replied, "I don't like English being called their second language!" And she never did.

Second grade brought us Juan Arriola from the far west. He was open to new ideas and he put tremendous effort into creating "learning centers". Basically, these were stations set up all around the room with activities to complete at each station. English and Spanish speaking youngsters were paired to assist language learning as peer mentors. Both parents and students enjoyed the freedom and it was an introduction to independent learning. By grades three we had Wilson Soto and his sister Nancy on board. They were former bilingual program participants who went on to the University of Connecticut and returned to Windham. Wilson had a flair for drama and the children became adept at acting in two languages. A production of Snow White in Spanish was a highlight of that year, with the only drawback 90-degree temperatures and kids in rabbit suits. Another classroom teacher, Mario Montes, entered with a bit to learn but his learning curve was immense and bolstered by his love of children. His third grade classroom scored highest on North Windham's CMT scores one year.

While Dual Language moved on, the new arrivals moved in. The Dual Language program kept its integrity for the moment, restricting program entry to those who started and grew through the program. Sometimes, the entry of a newcomer who had minimal English was approved. But the children came to Windham and the traditional program was necessary.

Both programs existed side by side. The Compañeros program now operated in two schools and it had reached the elementary school ending point at 4th grade. The new Windham Middle School had opened and there was space for the Dual Language program to move up. I wrote a grant to the Federal government Office of Education to assist in the expansion of the program and we were successful in getting this funding.

The funding helped hire some supplementary personnel, including a community liaison. We had several wonderful women in the past for the bilingual program but the dual language program went into the unknown with a young man, new to Windham. Alexi Colon was a marvelous musician and he had a philosophy that believed in the power of music to reach everyone. His mastery of the quattro led to performances by himself and by the children that impressed a variety of audiences. He wrote a special song for Compañeros and when all the children from all the Compañeros classrooms got together and sang their own song as one, no listener left untouched. Over two hundred children sang at the last event I attended, we came a long way. Alexi also brought back the paranda, a traveling music group similar to our Christmas carolers. Except for the Latin beat, they were the same in warmth. One late night after Christmas my husband and I sprang from our beds to see what was the matter. It was a paranda. The scramble for food and drink was invigorating and it became a night to remember, lasting until the last crumb was eaten by the music makers who ranged in age from five to fifty.

I never lacked for good advice. One young parent came to give me some relating to Alexi, our new community worker for the program. Alexi was a musician, skilled in the Quattro and in composition. He assembled a choir of children singing songs of trust in both English and Spanish. His programs were electric. For the other part of his position he was sent out to homes as his predecessors had been, to bring news of a child's progress or back-sliding and to offer support from town agencies. The difference between our former motherly community workers and Alexi was undeniable and I was advised to stop sending him to homes when the man of the house was not in his home. We planned school visits instead.

The funds that supported early dual language programs in Connecticut became more difficult to obtain and finally, they were gone. Windham was lucky to be part of the surge towards a new vision in the first stages of recognition in Connecticut. When I retired from Windham I worked as a consultant with other districts to enhance their dual language programs and they all became part of the future of the state as they had in other places with large minority language populations. As a tool for integration, there is still no better method: all parents and students had the goal of bilingualism and all were equal in the learning process.

A side benefit of Dual Language in Connecticut was the response of the State Legislature. Although the research was plentiful at this time, change was coming. Years of controversy resulted in an overhaul of bilingual education rules and regulations. A 30-month restriction was placed on enrollment in bilingual programs. ESL was the State's answer to newcomers. By the time this became a concern to educators it was well into the process of becoming law. However, time had given Windham enough data to show the results of Dual Language programs on students, and with this data in hand, the State exempted learners in Dual Language programs from the 30- month limit.

PROFESSIONAL DEVELOPMENT IN THE FIRST YEARS

In 1994-95, the University of Connecticut held a Summer Institute titled Teaching Linguistically and Culturally Diverse Learners. The program was sponsored by the

National Center for Research on Cultural Diversity and Second Language Learning and the presenters, Eugene Garcia and Donna Christian were experts in the field. They knew the questions to ask and had research to answer many of them. This set the tone for many Bilingual Program Directors in Connecticut as we planned the start of the school year. Windham's schedule for the year began with the general, Dealing With Multi-Level Abilities in the Classroom for all staff. In the same month, the State Department of Education brought Donna Christian from CAL, Marcela Von Vacano from the Key School in Arlington, Virginia and a language arts consultant from Connecticut. This was open to all administrators across the state.

From November through April, the Windham teachers, staff and parents were again scheduled to visit the Amigos program in Cambridge, Massachusetts, and also programs in Framingham and Salem. It was considered imperative that Windham educators and parents had an opportunity to see the different programs successfully operating in the area.

In the spring, the Multicultural Resource Center sponsored a workshop on Second Language Acquisition for the entire New England Region. Project Academy at Brown University produced a program called Training For Change Agents in the Schools presented by Dr. Robert Parker and Jane Yedlin, both remarkable for their practical approach. This last one described was specifically designed to reach superintendents bringing district teams.

The list gives an idea of the tremendous surge of information, organization and out-reach that educated the educators. All of the above were at no cost to participants except for the University Institute.We surely need another focus by Universities, State Departments of Education and Districts.

In addition to the major presenters, Windham held a full schedule of in-service with presenters from local Universities, other districts and Windham's own staff.

In 2008 I had the good fortune to become a student teacher observer in the North Windham Elementary School Compañeros program. Eastern Connecticut State University had placed a bilingual under-graduate with Eva Jimenez, a calm and competent first grade teacher. The program had changed format, following the model used in other districts. The children met with two teachers in weekly cycles: one teacher used English only; the second teacher headed the Spanish speaking room. All of the children were amazingly fluent in both languages. In the Spanish room where I observed, no English was spoken. The lessons were rich with vocabulary in context and the curriculum mirrored the instructional plans of all the 1st grade classrooms. Materials were plentiful; the room was organized for learning. Most interesting, the small groups were not homogenous by language but by learning objectives,

North Windham had become the Dual Language School with the teaching expertise, materials, curriculum, format and sequence needed to reach the original goal of bilingual, bicultural and biliterate students.

The last classes are shown in the next pictures.

A PORTRAIT IN TIME:
THE 1996 COMPAÑEROS
CLASSROOMS
GRADES K-4

WINDHAM CENTER SCHOOL
KINDERGARTEN A.M.
TEACHER: MIRIAN REYNOSO right
AIDE: LINDA DOMINGUEZ left

KINDERGARTEN P.M.
WINDHAM CENTER SCHOOL
TEACHER: MIRIAM REYNOSO Left Top
AIDE: LINDA DOMINGUEZ Right Top

In 2010, Mrs. Reynoso teaches Kindergarten and Grade 1 in the Windham Center Bilingual Program. She has the ability to move many students into mainstream classes quickly and successfully. For the past few years, the school has implemented looping, giving some children two consecutive years of attention. She is truly a gifted teacher with the knack for having an organized class and happy children.

Ms. Dominguez lives in Willimantic and is a devoted grandmom. She was a steady hand in the classroom with a strong tie to the children and parents she served.

GRADE 1: TEACHER: YUSOMIL BONET Left
AIDE: RAQUEL PEREZ

Ms. Bonet is still as dedicated and energetic as she was playing Mozart in her Kindergarten class many years ago. It worked, her class was always mellow! Her ability to organize events is appreciated at Windham Middle School where she holds the position of Transition Teacher. Her students include newcomers, bilingual program students and Compañeros participants who need support from a bilingual teacher.

GRADE 2: TEACHER: MAYRA CRUZ right
AIDE: DIANE PRUE left
READING SUPPORT: PAT SHIMCHICK center

Ms. Cruz left Connecticut for Florida but she is still in touch with teachers from Windham. She is remembered as a fine teacher with an outstanding voice that brought our concerts to a perfect pitch.

Mrs. Shimchick is now a therapist and those who knew her work with children will know that now, she is able to deal with any stress that her clients bring to her office.

GRADE 2: NORTH WINDHAM SCHOOL
TEACHER: CAROL PALADINO right
AIDE: BETSY ARVELO left

Ms. Paladino has since married and left the Windham Schools. Ms. Arvelo is with us still but working at the Windham Middle School. She demonstrates the same energy today that she brought to dodge ball at Sweeney Elementary School as a student.

GRADE 3: NORTH WINDHAM SCHOOL
TEACHER: MARIO MONTES

Mr. Montes came to Windham from Mexico. His classes did well year after year, surpassing those of mainstream third grade students. He passed away several years ago and is missed by all who knew him.

*GRADE 4: NORTH WINDHAM SCHOOL
TEACHER: WILSON SOTO*

Mr. Soto came back to the Windham Public Schools to teach in the program after completing his degrees at the University of Connecticut. He has since moved to New Jersey and is the author of several books about Puerto Rico and its legends. His interest in drama continues, he is a born showman.

One class is missing from the picture. Crista Demers was the partner of Yusomil Bonet in grade 1. She was a great addition to the group.

The program was located in two schools: Windham Center was home to K-1 and North Windham to grades 2-4. In 5th grade, they were all joined together at Windham Middle School.

When I retired from Windham, Compañeros had grown to include all of the elementary grades. I wrote a grant to bring the program to Windham Middle School and it was funded. It was harder to leave than I expected and so I begged to be allowed to stay another year as Project Director of the new grant, bringing the Dual Language program to grade 5. After many years of interesting offices I moved to a spacious room in the new school. The transition to middle school went smoothly because of the quality of our teachers and the continuity planned and executed with grant funds. There have been many changes to the original design but there is still a program at Windham Middle School and it has some of the best teachers in the building. The former Grade 1 teacher, Yusomil Bonet, is now a Transition Teacher at the Middle School. She joins Madeline Negron, Principal, in creating and teaching dance and music to the traveling group of artists from the school.

As we talked about the beginnings of the Compañeros program in November, 2010, Ms. Bonet noted that she kept the list of high school graduates each year and highlighted those from the dual language program for her own satisfaction. They have done well.

Prologue and Conclusions

The socio-linguistics of bilingual education are far too complicated to explain to those in power who still work with the folk wisdom of the past. The reliance on long ago immigrant anecdotes did not take into account the movement of our society from agriculture to technology and the need for education to allow new arrivals to compete. Each situation for school districts in the USA was different: no one size model would serve all. Some of the variables include the linguistic competence of the target population, the status of the second language in the society, the learning style of the minority language group, the size of the minority group and, finally, the economic value of the minority language. Nevertheless, no bilingual educator that I knew rejected the need for students to learn English. The question was always how to learn English without learning only English.

Questions asked ten years ago, and more, are still being asked today. Conferences have largely been replaced by webcasts and on-line chats. Grant funds are distributed to states for disbursement. The Government is active but not as involved. At a recent round table at the University of Connecticut, practitioners brought up the lack of support by administration and fellow teachers, students with potential but personal problems that interfered with learning, and difficult transitions for receiving teachers in the mainstream. They sounded all too familiar although we have come a long way from the '70's. This country will not be as great as it could be without the full enfranchisement of all its children. The loss of even one subtracts from the total pool of talent within our boundaries.

My reason for writing is to remember the students and events that were a large part of my life, and to make some sense out of the successes and failures. It was a great moment when the 1990 census reported five of my former students on the rolls of homeowners in Windham. The possibilities inherent in a solid middle class Latino population are many. The involvement in town governance is established, the Latino teachers are many and a former bilingual program student beautifully handles the role of administrator.

The Dual Language program thrives: it is in its seventeenth year. A possible drawback, solved only by teacher dedication, is the daily barrage of English at school and at home. When all are English speakers, Spanish as the medium for functioning in the classroom has to be guarded well by the teacher responsible for that component. Parent support continues and it is doubtful that the program will disappear in Windham as it has in Hartford.

Many of my former students are working in service jobs, especially for the elderly and mentally challenged. Others went on to professional positions in education. And some are gone. A super star of the community died in September 2009 at the age of 43 after many years of treatment for kidney disease. He had a B.A. in Art History and French Literature and an M.A. in education. Most of all, he was dedicated to the community. His leadership focused on opportunities for those following him in the quest for full participation in the society at large. Fernando Olmo is a name to remember and anyone who knew him will have memories of what can be accomplished by one person. He took the best from life each day and always looked ahead to greater challenges.

Every one of the students I knew over 25 years in Windham had potential. The same is true for English language learners today.

In 2010, the Windham Public Schools in northeast Connecticut continue to offer a successful Spanish-English Dual Language Program and a Transitional Bilingual Program for students entering the district at any grade level without the English needed to participate in mainstream classrooms.

The early graduates of Compañeros, the Dual Language Program, achieve academic success whether they began knowing only English or only Spanish. In any case, they realize that cultural differences are not barriers to friendship. The full development of Spanish by English speakers did not quite work as planned. English overwhelmed the Spanish speakers and English became their choice in most situations. It wasn't planned to happen, but dual language was instrumental in hastening the acquisition of English.

Today, bilingual teachers in programs designed to help children learn content and language are not separate nor are their skills and talents marginalized. The teachers are supervised by the same principals who observe their colleagues, they participate in the same professional development activities and they help their students master the same curriculum.

Administrators have also moved on. In districts with high incidence English language learners, supervision is often based on the Sheltered Instruction Observation Protocol (SIOP), a method of instruction suited to the needs of second Language Learners. In short, SIOP is a method of helping children learn content as well as language. In many urban districts, it is clear that this particular protocol works equally well for many children, even those whose only language is English.

As in the past, the most difficult issues are found clustered around students in the middle school and high school. The range of entry-level skills in the first language is significant with older students who may have moved many times before entering mainland public schools. Their background knowledge does not mesh with the curriculum of their peers. Indeed, the sequence of mathematics alone presents a problem for late entries: it is not the same as in the USA. A principal noted with concern that Advanced Placement courses at the high school were lacking English language learners or Latinos. While many Latino students are in the mainstream, their exit from bilingual programs may be recent or they may not have had any transition into mainland schools. When

I taught English as a Second Language at Windham High School in the late '70's and early '80's the students who did best were those who came prepared in Spanish content. Although their English might be limited, their academics were not. The English language came through as a transfer of content and many moved on to University. They may have required more time to complete their degrees but they achieved undergraduate and graduate diplomas.

It would be an extraordinary pleasure to report that there has been a steady movement towards addressing the needs of English language learners. In some cases we have moved back to our beginnings in the '50's, before the passage of the 1964 Civil Rights Act began to put a legal face on classroom practices. While "high expectations" became a mantra in the public schools, well meaning teachers allow minority language children to believe they are performing well when, in fact, they are below standards set for their peers. Major problems remain. In 1994 I presented the following concerns as issues: Pre-school programs that utilize the language of the children served; remedial support staff who know the children's language; trained staff knowledgeable in content areas they teach; adequate funding for materials and technology; integration of bilingual program staff and students into all district and school action plans, and the training of all teachers in the theory and practice of second language acquisition. I would probably list the same issues in 2010.

The journey over the past four decades was not a continuous progression towards solutions. At times then and now in Connecticut and other states, bilingual education was jettisoned in favor of English only. My own belief in Bilingual Education developed over the years in Windham, watching to see if the best and brightest really could find success and whether all the children had a chance to learn in the public schools. Our record could be better.

November, 2010